THE CONDUCTOR'S ART

THE
CONDUCTOR'S ART

by

WARWICK BRAITHWAITE
F.R.A.M.

GREENWOOD PRESS, PUBLISHERS
WESTPORT, CONNECTICUT

Library of Congress Cataloging in Publication Data

Braithwaite, Henry Warwick, 1896-1971.
    The conductor's art.

        Reprint of the 1952 ed. published by Williams
    and Norgate, London.
            1. Conducting.   I.   Title.
    MT85.B8   1978   781.6'35   77-25407
    ISBN 0-313-20058-0

First published 1952

Reprinted with the permission of R. Q. Braithwaite

Reprinted in 1978 by Greenwood Press, Inc.
51 Riverside Avenue, Westport, CT 06880

Printed in the United States of America

PREFACE

ONE MAY well ask why I feel called upon to write a book on conducting. There are several reasons, most of them for myself alone. In fact, it might be said that I wrote this manual for myself, but I would add that if it helps the young conductor in his problems then I have done some little good. Apart from this, the main reason why I submit this manual to students is that it seems to me that there has not been written a book which gives a definite plan for the development of the technique of conducting.

Many conductors have studied at schools with another conductor and acquired their technique through the experience of others in this way. But it is a lamentable fact that few, if any, great conductors have written a book on the subject or have had the inclination or time to teach others. Many of them are self-taught! Even if they could give the time to teaching it is doubtful whether they could be expected to go through the laborious task of teaching the arm movements to students. They can best be heard, and in that way teach those of us who are willing to learn.

I am of the opinion that just as instrumentalists learn their scales and arpeggios and their technique before venturing out as artists, the conductor ought to learn the arm movements of his art before trying the patience of orchestral players or at least those of them who know their job. Apart from this, so long as a conductor is continually worried by technique he will not always be able to bring off during performance his ideas as to interpretation.

I have assumed that the student has already mastered the elementary technique of conducting—if not, I recommend Sir Adrian Boult's treatise *A Handbook on the Technique of Conducting*, which is concise, to the point, and very valuable from a student's point of view.

Finally I want to thank the following publishers for permission to quote from the works listed:—

Messrs. Novello & Co. Ltd.—Ballet Music *The Perfect Fool*
by Holst
United Music Publishers Ltd.—*L'Après-Midi d'un Faune* by
Debussy.
Messrs. Boosey & Hawkes Ltd.—*Die Foteninsel* by Rachmani-
noff and *Le Sacre du Printemps* by Stravinsky.

London,   W. B.
January, 1952

CONTENTS

PART III

Opera

PART I

THE PHYSICAL MOVEMENTS

Chapter I

INTRODUCTORY

AN INSTRUMENTALIST who sets out to perform a musical work without having mastered technique or without having acquired at least a good grounding in technique is doomed to failure from the outset. The more difficult the technical problems the greater his fall from grace.

But how much more important is it that a conductor, dealing with a collection of different personalities comprising an orchestra, should know all the problems connected with his art in order that the composer's intentions should reach the ears of his listeners in as faithful an interpretation as reasonably possible.

The conductor is dealing with (in a good orchestra) a collection of men and women each expert in his or her own sphere. A player is expected to play his instrument well—otherwise he wouldn't be in an orchestra. If a player's technique fails him at rehearsal he still has an opportunity of practising and may overcome his difficulties. If his technique fails him at performance and such failure occurs several times he is replaced by a better man.

In other words, only the highest standards are tolerated from an instrumentalist in an orchestra. From a conductor the least that is expected is that his technique should be flawless. Having acquired a flawless technique of beating time he will always get a good performance. The measure of his greatness as an artist-conductor is another question entirely. The acquisition of a flawless technique is only the beginning of conducting. Musicianship, interpretive powers, an impeccable ear: all these qualities, if the initial gifts are there, can be improved with good teaching.

Personality and the power to sway a body of players to the highest realms of great music-making are another matter. Personality, that indefinable quality, cannot be taught. Yet without it, in some form or other, a conductor will remain where he started—on the lowest rung of the ladder. On the other hand great driving power, coupled with interpretive gifts of a high order, plus good musicianship, will enable a would-be conductor (not without set-backs, sometimes of a distressing nature) to improve himself through experience—if he can get it or persuade an orchestra to let him have it!

To help the young conductor to avoid such set-backs is the object of this book.

CHAPTER II

IRREGULAR DIVISIONS OF THE BAR

AFTER acquiring the arm movements of the simpler varieties of time-signatures there remain the much more difficult problems of what I call "irregular" bar lengths in which the time length of the beats in any given bar are unequal. These "irregular" bars are never easy. They often come so suddenly and are over so quickly and are so mixed up, often with "regular" beats, that it is essential, before rehearsing one of these works for the first time, that the conductor should be so far advanced in his practice that such technical problems present no difficulty and that his beats should be absolutely clear to the players.

If there is one thing that bores and wearies orchestral players it is the conductor who has to "learn" his technique on them. Rehearsals become maddening, players groan inwardly (sometimes even audibly), nerves are frayed, and the conductor becomes physically and mentally exhausted. This can all be avoided, and at the risk of repeating myself over and over again, I ask that the "Morning Practice" exercises at the end of this and other chapters be practised until they become "second nature".

Perhaps the most difficult aspect in these days of the conductor's art, technically, is the conducting of modern music abounding in irregular time-signatures. The freedom of the modern composer knows no bounds, and although one may be convinced that quite a lot of the experimental music written will not live, yet a conductor must be prepared to pilot an orchestra through intricacies (although musically not worth the trouble!) of an almost superhuman nature. One is comforted by the knowledge that, with the majority of these works, once the complexities have been mastered there is little else to worry about. But apart from his own estimation of certain modern composers it is a conductor's duty to give all well-written works a trial, for the conductor stands midway between composer and public, and thus should exercise as unbiased an attitude as he is personally capable of.

The most difficult irregular time-signature is the quick $\frac{5}{8}$ or $\frac{7}{8}$ very often strewn by modern composers among normal but fast regular bars. There is the fast $\frac{3}{8}$ also. At the time of writing, I have not yet come across the fast $\frac{11}{8}$ or $\frac{13}{8}$ but it is quite likely there are a few examples of this.

(i) For $\frac{3}{8}$ the arm movement required is the quick down beat —one in a bar. By itself this represents no difficulty, but when followed or preceded by (in a fast piece) a $\frac{2}{4}$ bar and sometimes a $\frac{3}{4}$, the sudden lengthening of the pulse beat in the $\frac{3}{8}$ is a real difficulty for some people. By the "pulse beat" I mean the fundamental note length of the beat. Some works are "felt" in crotchets all through; some in quavers. It is largely a matter of convenience and personal feeling. Sometimes it might be wise and safer to feel a movement all through in the quaver pulse thus helping one in the awkward changes from regular to irregular bars.

An interesting work to study as an example of this is William Walton's overture *Portsmouth Point*, but the following exercise is recommended before actually studying the overture.

(quaver pulse) $\frac{2}{4}|\frac{3}{4}|\frac{3}{8}|\frac{2}{4}|\frac{3}{8}|\frac{3}{4}|\frac{2}{4}|\frac{3}{8}|\frac{2}{4}$

We will leave further consideration of this point in the chapter on "mixing".

(ii) The next time-signature to be considered is the fast $\frac{5}{8}$ bar rhythmically divided into $\frac{2}{8}$ and $\frac{3}{8}$. The arm movements are the short down and the long up beat. There is also the $\frac{5}{8}$ with the bar divided into $\frac{3}{8}$ and $\frac{2}{8}$. Practise the exercises given at the end of this chapter under the title "Morning Practice". The conductor should sing the exercises while conducting.

(iii) The next time-signature is the more difficult fast $\frac{7}{8}$ divided into $\frac{4}{8}$ and $\frac{3}{8}$ or $\frac{3}{8}$ and $\frac{4}{8}$. The arm movements are almost identical with the above, but of course the beats are in each case longer. Practise with the quavers always at the same tempo and sing the notes at the same time. (See "Morning Practice", page 15.)

(iv) Very often the $\frac{7}{8}$ is divided into $\frac{2}{8}$, $\frac{2}{8}$, $\frac{3}{8}$ with variations in the rhythm of $\frac{3}{8}$, $\frac{2}{8}$, $\frac{2}{8}$ or $\frac{2}{8}$, $\frac{3}{8}$, $\frac{2}{8}$. Practise these variations, always remembering that the quaver has the same value and that the beat for the $\frac{3}{8}$, wherever it is, is longer than the $\frac{2}{8}$. An excellent example of $\frac{7}{8}$ is contained in de Falla's *El Amor Brujo*, on page 79 (full score).

The above remarks also apply to fast $\frac{3}{4}$, $\frac{5}{4}$, and $\frac{7}{4}$. In the case of a slow tempo the beat is quite straightforward except that the long portions of the bar must be noted and the beat adjusted accordingly.[1]

[1] The one important point to remember is that in *every* bar length, regular or irregular, there must always be a strong down beat at the beginning of *each* bar.

MORNING PRACTICE

Instructions I. Sing each exercise while conducting.
II. Repeat each exercise four times.
III. When each exercise is mastered join them all together and repeat at least ten times.

IRREGULAR TIME-SIGNATURES

$\quad=126$ (or faster)   (short—long beats)

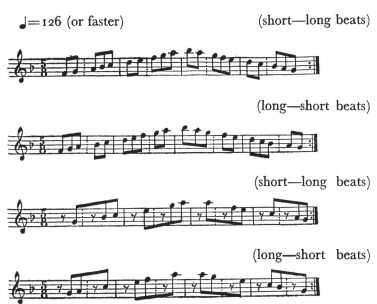

(long—short beats)

(short—long beats)

(long—short beats)

(1 long—2 short beats)

(2 short—1 long beat)

(1 short—1 long—1 short beat)

(1 long—1 very long)

(1 short—1 long—1 short beat)

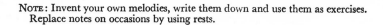

NOTE: Invent your own melodies, write them down and use them as exercises.
Replace notes on occasions by using rests.

CHAPTER III

MIXING REGULAR WITH IRREGULAR TIME-SIGNATURES

Now WE come to the study of the most difficult technical problems. The "mixing" of irregular bars occurs to a great extent in modern music and the student cannot be too expert in this side of his technique.

I recommend that the exercises given at the end of this chapter should be sung and conducted every morning for at least half an hour, even when the conductor has passed out of the student stage. In this way the ease of arm movements (or in some cases, wrist movements) will be cultivated and retained. For it must be remembered that the conductor should always give clear beats to the players. Airy wanderings in mid-air are not appreciated by orchestral artists. On the other hand technique should never be allowed to interfere with concentration on the music during the performance. All technique should become "second nature" and not till this *is* so will the performance be smooth and satisfying.

A warning to the student is not out of place here. Extravagance of gesture should be shunned. All movements should be easy to look at and as "small" as the distance between players and conductor will permit. During performance one's natural tendency is to get excited and under the stress of feeling and warmth the arm movements will become more pronounced. One should aim at saving one's energy for the big moments; not only the *one big moment*—this is unnatural and savours of preciousness—but all in due proportion.

There are many moments in big works where one's energy can be used almost to the full yet there may only be one great climax. For this climax a certain amount of strength should be saved. But nothing is more annoying both to players and audience than when a conductor rigidly controls his "feelings" all through the work only to become restive out of all proportion in the great climax. It is almost as if he says, "Look! All that has gone before was as nothing, but *this* moment I really feel is worth a little extra exertion on my part." This is quite wrong and most unnatural when we think how the composer must have "burned with an inner fire" during the composition of every bar, and it is almost an act of public vandalism.

In this matter the student will think for himself. It is useless to follow blindly any one interpretation. *The proof of any method is the result attained.* Dry and unfeeling leadership in music never produced worth-while results yet, and a conductor is dealing with flesh and blood both in the orchestra and audience: he must burn with a fiery zeal for music. This, backed up by true artistic feeling and musicianship, plus a solid study of technique, will produce the right kind of results.

The first "mixing" for practice is the $\frac{5}{8}$ and the $\frac{6}{8}$. Once the preliminary exercises following Chapter II have been mastered no further explanation is necessary. The student must practise the exercises in each section before going on to the next group. This is essential, and indeed such a course of training as I have outlined will be utterly useless unless the student keeps rigidly to it.

The student should practise each exercise, mastering them one by one until he memorises them. Later he should combine two or more exercises together and eventually go through the whole series several times without a stop. One word of warning: It is better to study with a conductor of experience so that he can watch over the progress of the student and correct any fault in his style. Some students will have little difficulty in grasping the whole scheme of exercises at a glance, but (and here I would add a stronger warning) mere "grasp" of the method and the details do not constitute finality of achievement. Before the muscles of the arm and wrist are our willing servants there must be a great deal of practice given over a long period. If one is so fortunate as to be "born" into the position of a conductor of an orchestra giving concerts every day or even every other day, then one can give one's method actual trial and one's muscles should become day by day more used to the strain put upon them. If one hasn't clear ideas about technique one's conducting is apt to become angular and unrestful, soon transmitted to the players, making for a rough performance. As a guide to the student I would recommend two points for him *in performance*:

(1) Be as restful in your movements as possible in quiet moments.

(2) Get your effect and your meaning over to the orchestra by whatever means in your power.

We are not all of the same mould. Some are naturally restful, undemonstrative, although fine musicians and perhaps feeling everything acutely. On the other hand violence out of all proportion is quite disgusting to look at, and the student cannot be warned too strongly to avoid it. If he is given to extravagance of movement he must alter his style as soon as possible. The only cure for this is practising as quietly as possible even in the robust movements. But before inflicting this on your audience try it out in the privacy of your own study. I have reserved fuller discussion of this and other points for Part II. In the meantime, I suggest the student gets his mind clear on all technical points as regards the arm movements of conducting.

The following exercises should be sung and conducted each morning even when they have been mastered, as they form a valuable aid in easing the arm muscles.

In each exercise take the quaver as always equal to the following quavers. At first the exercises should be taken through at a moderate pace—say $\quarternote=88$—and from that comparatively slow pace work up to $\quarternote=126$ or faster.

MIXING IRREGULAR BAR LENGTHS

Instructions. I. Repeat each exercise four times singing the notes at the same time as conducting.

II. Vary the exercises by inventing phrases with notes of longer length taking a whole beat.

III. Replace notes on occasions by using rests.

After mastering each exercise combine the series going through the whole system without a stop (making no repeats).

Keep the length of the quavers firmly in your mind.

♩ = 126 (or faster)

Keep the length of the quavers firmly in your mind.

(in $\frac{7}{8}$ 1 long and 2 short)

(in $\frac{7}{8}$ 1 long and 1 not so long.)

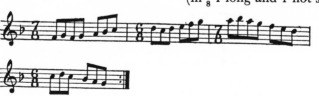

NOTE: All these exercises must be sung by the student while conducting. By singing the exercises the student will be inclined to think of them melodically, thus combining technique with actual melody.

Chapter IV

SUDDEN CHANGES OF TIME

By SUDDEN changes of time I mean the sudden change from one bar to another of totally different beat value, where the pulse may or may not be the same. This kind of change is frequently met with in modern music and requires a great deal of steadiness on the part of player and conductor.

I will deal with those changes where the "pulse" is of the same value in both time-signatures.

(1) The most frequent form of this is the ₵ and $\frac{3}{4}$ which is met so frequently in Strauss's works. The change of time involved is the equivalent of $\frac{2}{4}$ followed by $\frac{3}{8}$ already mentioned in Chapter II but whereas the latter has generally been applied to running quaver figures it is often split up in a most complicated manner and consequently the pulse beat is somewhat slower. There are several examples of this change, but two will suffice. The $\frac{3}{4}$ bar in Strauss's tone poem *Don Juan* (page 7, full score) and the continuous change in *Salome* (pages 12 to 15, piano score). The pulse is, of course, the crochet in these cases and the value of this pulse must be kept in mind. On the other hand one conducts these pages with two-minim beats in the alla breve and the one short and one long in the $\frac{5}{4}$ (rather like the $\frac{5}{8}$ mentioned before).

(See "Morning Practice" at end of this chapter for this and following examples.)

(2) Next we must consider a change which presents a certain difficulty—the change from ₵ to $\frac{6}{8}$. A notable example of this is the finale of Schubert's *Rosamunde*. (I once heard this taken at a speed in the $\frac{6}{8}$ of ♪ = ♩ of previous bar which of course really makes it $\frac{6}{4}$.) Actually I feel I am right in saying that the ♩ = ♩. is correct: in other words the same length of bar in both cases.

The main thing to be decided is the pace of the ♩. in the $\frac{6}{8}$. Usually the composer gives ♩. = ♩ of previous bar in which case there is nothing to worry about.

The only possible difficulty is if the composer means the ⁶₈ to be as a little faster ⁶₄ in which case the ♩ does not equal the ♩. and the *pulse* value is not the same. This kind of difficulty is rare but it is well to practise it so that you are prepared for it when it comes.

(3) All of these changes are difficult only if the conductor is not fully conscious of the new tempo but apart from this it is essential to train the wrist and arm to obey the mind instantly. In fact one of the chief difficulties of the young conductor is the indicating of new tempo. Often, in the excitement of the movement, a young conductor will beat wildly almost any tempo. This is largely due to lack of steadiness on his part and must be overcome at all costs. A valuable help to this is the thorough rehearsal every morning of the complete cycle of exercises given in this chapter but with special references to the difficulty in hand. In the final chapter a mode of morning study is suggested dealing with actual examples.

(4) The next change for consideration is the ⁴₄ followed by ⁶₄. This is only difficult on rare occasions. The point to be considered is whether the ♩=♩ or the ♩.=♩ of the previous bar. Once this point is clear the conducting of it is a fairly easy matter. But sometimes this *can* present considerable difficulty, more especially the change back again to the slow ⁶₄. In this respect it will be interesting to consider the opening of Debussy's *La Mer*, and I propose to deal with this at some length.

At figure 2 (miniature score) the beat is normally two in a bar which very soon quickens until the ⁶₈ is reached and at this point the beat becomes a quaver six in a bar. To give the required tempo at the ⁶₈ is not so easy as it looks, and requires a very definite idea and great steadiness. I am sure that some people may find this change comparatively easy. On the other hand others caught up imaginatively by the sweeping accelerando may find it difficult to drop back to the slow tranquil tempo of the ⁶₈. This is a point which should be practised by the student by means of the example given at the end of this chapter, after which try it out with the Debussy score in front of you.

(5) Next there is the ordinary difficulty of the very fast ²₄ in which there is an occasional ³₄ bar. If the tempo of the ²₄ is so fast that one in a bar is the normal beat, then the ³₄ becomes increasingly difficult. I would recommend there a very quick

three beats in the $\frac{3}{4}$, or if too fast for that, a down beat swerved to the right (after reaching its point), with a continuing movement upwards in readiness for the next $\frac{2}{4}$ "one-in-a-bar" beat.

An example of this can be seen in the Dohnanyi *Ruralia Hungarica*, 2nd movement. These movements should be practised a number of times using the exercise given at end of this section. In these quick tempi, use the wrist movement only, otherwise the tempo may tend to become ponderous.

Next, $\frac{6}{8}$ and $\frac{3}{4}$, a very frequently used change. The chief things to remember in this change is that the ♪ = ♪ and be careful that the ♩. beat never gets faster than its three quaver length. The difficulty is not a great one.

(6) And, lastly, the change from allegro $\frac{4}{4}$ or ¢ to grave $\frac{4}{4}$ (or $\frac{8}{8}$).

There is nothing difficult about this except that the mind must be clear as to the pace of the quaver in the $\frac{8}{8}$. The Haydn, Handel, and Mozart overtures and symphonies, etc., abound in examples of this change.

Often one will find in Mozart, Haydn and other early composers that after the introduction in $\frac{8}{8}$ the Allegro that follows is too fast for four beats and must be in two (Alla Breve). Again this is a question of making up one's mind beforehand.

(7) *Sudden changes of time-signatures, but where the rhythm or melody remains the same.*

This can occur in two ways:

(i) When the rhythm or tune of a previous movement begins to show itself in the present movement in readiness for a return to the original at the change of time-signature.

In this case care must be taken that the tempo of the present movement should be just right so that the old tune in its new guise will be played at the correct tempo. Examples of this are numerous. (For instance, in *Hansel and Gretel* at the end, after the witch has been pushed into the oven and the children dance a wild waltz, the rhythm appears in the previous $\frac{9}{8}$, one beat of which becomes a bar of the $\frac{3}{4}$ so that ♩ = ♪ of the previous bar. Another example is the Bizet "Carillon" towards the end of the $\frac{6}{8}$ in which the bell theme is played by the horns and should be played so that the change at the $\frac{3}{4}$ is imperceptible.

There are many examples of this vice versa—where three bars of $\frac{3}{4}$ are equal to one bar of $\frac{9}{8}$. Care must be taken that the

♪=♩ An example of this is "Siegfried's Journey to the Rhine" but in this case the ⁹⁄₈ is used because of the Rhinegold theme which is a three-pulse rhythm theme. Of course there is no question of the new tune appearing in the ³⁄₄ here, but there is the definite rhythm which is carried on into the ⁹⁄₈.

(ii) When a doppio piu lento occurs and the figure of the previous movement is carried on into the next, the only difference is that the value of the written note is different. The example of this I have in mind occurs in the Scherzo of Sibelius's *Fourth Symphony*. (Page 22, full score, letter K, doppio piu lento.)

It will be observed that the time signature does not alter and that the doppio piu lento is not strictly correct in this case. This example is an interesting one in that the ♩=♩ of the previous bar—*not*, you will observe, ♩.=♩ The chief difficulty is breaking into the correct tempo (three beats in a bar) at the doppio piu lento so that the ♪=♪ of previous bar. That is a matter for great steadiness and should be practised with great care.

Another very interesting example of sudden changes of tempo is the slow movement of Mahler's *Fourth Symphony* from figure 19 right on to the end of the movement.

Personally I have always found Rachmaninoff's *Die Toten Insel* a problem in this respect. The composer has marked ♩ ♩. taktieren, at the speed of ♩=60, which means that the first beat being ♩=60 the second is ♩.=40. Now at first this is comparatively easy even although the quaver =120. But later on when the music becomes more involved (and 120=♪ is not an awkwardly quick beat) I have often commenced with quaver beats partly to help myself out as well as the players. Care, however, must be taken to go back to the two beats when five are not necessary otherwise the tempo may become a little ponderous. Later the tempo becomes faster and two beats are necessary, but here it is easier by reason of the increase in the pace. However this is a problem which must be solved and I would recommend exercises No. I and II at the end of Section 3 to be practised at ♩=60 (or ♪=120) as much as possible.

Continue your practice into the ⁷⁄₈ with ♩ ♩ ♩. beats. An example of this which is really worth a great deal of study because of the problems leading up to it is the ballet music from

Holst's *The Perfect Fool*. Here at the $\frac{7}{8}$ the tempo is not given, with the exception of the rather doubtful expression "moderato". To make matters more difficult Holst has commenced the movement with an andanto $\frac{3}{4}$ followed by a $\frac{9}{8}$ and $\frac{6}{8}$, where the ♩.=♩ of the $\frac{3}{4}$. Then after a number of $\frac{6}{8}$ bars at ♩.=♩ (of $\frac{3}{4}$) he puts in a $\frac{1}{4}$ bar (♪=♪) immediately before the $\frac{7}{8}$. Now the question is, is the ♩ of the $\frac{7}{8}$ equal to the ♩ of the $\frac{1}{4}$ or the ♩. of the $\frac{6}{8}$. The reason why I quote this rather fully is because it is absolutely essential that the conductor gives the correct and very steady tempo at the $\frac{7}{8}$ without any hesitation. The answer to the problem is that the tempo at the $\frac{7}{8}$ is ♩=♩ of $\frac{1}{4}$ and on playing or reading a little further on one sees in the tenth bar a group of semiquavers which undoubtedly give the tempo. The steadiness required first of all at the beginning of the $\frac{7}{8}$ is purely a question of knowing the tempo, but later, care must be taken that the quavers in the latter part of the bar (the $\frac{3}{8}$) are kept absolutely equal.

Extract from Holst's Ballet *Perfect Fool*.

Allegro   Moderato

Holst's works abound in problems of this sort and portions of *The Hymn of Jesus* where $\frac{5}{4}$ is followed by $\frac{5}{2}$ in rapid succession are worth studying purely from a technical point of view. Both these examples are taken faster than the pace of the $\frac{7}{8}$ (or $\frac{7}{4}$) we are discussing. When the pace is a moderate one the beat is easier to manage, but when it gets slower, then one must keep a steady hand on everyone, including oneself.

There is no royal road to success in the cultivation of steadiness. Some conductors have it born in them—nothing can move them (sometimes something should)—others cannot keep a steady tempo either in fast or slow movements. With some people it is a defect in their character and they become excited in the fiery moods, and unrestive in the tranquil ones. But the worst example is the bad musician who has no idea of time. If a student has any of these faults he must tear them out by the roots by a most vigorous method. The only advice I can give him is to practise every exercise very slowly—frequently testing himself with a metronome and going through all the exercises every morning. Then practise conducting an imaginary orchestra with a score in front of him of some adagio movement. If he does this *till he is cured*—frequently changing the work he conducts (in imagination) it will leave an indelible impression on his mind.

Lack of steadiness in fast movements is a fault which is also the result of excitability and a fiery nature. It leads to the great evil, in time, of taking everything too fast. There is no cure for this except frequent experience as a conductor— particularly with amateurs—when, if the conductor loses his head as well, there will be what is professionally known as a "dry-up" or complete breakdown and a dead stop—something a conductor will never forget should it ever happen to him in performance. An experience like this will probably teach him the value of holding his forces in check. On the other hand the conductor who holds his players in check so well that he only succeeds in securing a "lame" performance must get out of that bad habit also.

CHANGES OF TIME-SIGNATURES

I and II   Keep in mind the *length* (value) of crochet all through.

Sing this while conducting.

Take care that the ♩. beat in the $\frac{6}{8}$ is appreciably slower than the alla breve.

Keep control of your tempo at the return to ♪=116 (♩=116 of $\frac{6}{4}$).

Think all through of the crotchet.

Keep the quaver value firmly alive in your mind.

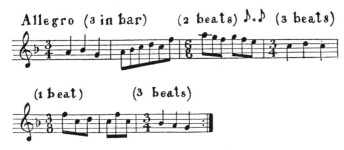

Settle in your mind the tempo of the Grave before you commence.

Before using this exercise decide firmly in your mind the two different tempi.

It is most important that you sing this exercise while conducting it. Strictly speaking it is not a bar length doppio
lento but a note length l'istesso tempo.

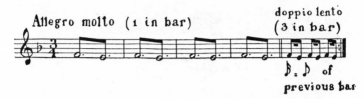

ADVANCED EXERCISES

EXERCISE I

NOTE: This is only *one* exercise and should be practised every morning, but only after all the previous exercises have been mastered. The quaver is the pulse value all through and the exercise is designed to give steadiness and control. After this exercise has been thoroughly mastered and memorized the tempo should be quickened until the student can conduct it changing in a crochet pulse, although in some bars he will have to think in a quaver pulse to keep his tempo steady. In dealing with the Alla breve a crochet beat will be much easier than a minim bea and the student is recommended to use this beat instead of the more difficult minim one.

ADVANCED EXERCISES

EXERCISE II

(adapted from *Die Toten Insel* by Rachmaninoff)

At * note the change to 3 and 2 quaver beats.

EXERCISE III

NOTE: This exercise exploits the change from ♩. pulse to the ♩ and care must be taken to give full value to these changes, especially the ♩.

C

EXERCISE IV

(adapted from *Le Sacre du Printemps* by Stravinsky)

EXERCISE V

NOTE: (a) After practising the two above exercises, study 'Le Sacre du Printemps' from page 112 (miniature score).

(b) For further and more complicated study of irregular time-signature work at figure 103 and onwards from the same work.

The quaver is the pulse beat all through these exercises. There are several "traps" which the student must memorize if he would avoid them. Take care of the $\frac{2}{16}$ bar when it occurs, it is unexpected and difficult after the succession of $\frac{3}{16}$'s.

CHAPTER V

SLOW TEMPI

THE PROBLEMS contained in quick tempi calling for quick realisation and instantaneous co-operation of mind and arm movements may be difficult for certain temperaments, but more often the problems of the slow tempi, especially with changing time-signature, can cause trouble.

In these passages, or bars sometimes, where there is nothing happening except perhaps a long held note for the first part of the bar with perhaps a theme of a few notes only at the end of the bar—in these bars a rigid control over one's natural tendencies must be strong indeed if the element of time value is to be kept. An example of what I mean is to be seen in the 1st movement of Sibelius's *Fourth Symphony*, bar 6, to letter A and letter B—and if steadiness needs to be acquired I advise practising this example fairly frequently. A further test for the conductor who lacks steadiness is also to be had in the 3rd movement of the same symphony which presents problems not only of steadiness but of technique as well. I will discuss these and other questions in the final chapter. Suffice it to say here that these problems are not solved by taking the music along at a faster pace than the composer obviously intended; on the other hand a futile beating of unnecessary beats in bars where the music seems to the listener almost to stand still, is useless and disturbing. But if you *do not* beat these unnecessary beats you *must beat them in your own mind,* and thus keep the feeling of time value. In doing this you will soon feel the correct pace of the movement and be able to regulate the tempi after one or two practices. This symphony is worth all the study a student can give it.

I propose now to deal with those slow tempi in which the conductor feels he is on the border line of doubt as to whether he should beat auxiliary beats or fundamental beats. In other words whether they should be "pulse" beats or not. In the last chapter I spoke of "pulse beats". Now when the tempi is fast—or *beyond a certain pace* (generally when too fast to beat fundamental beats) the beat value can be of greater length than the melody note so that a beat may be equal to several pulse values and thus the pulse note or value takes care of itself by reason of the fast movement. In slower tempi the pulse beat is much more evident and can be controlled with a beat all to itself as it were. But the question which troubles every conductor is "How and when should I divide up the beat?" The answer to this involves many considerations.

The practical problem facing conductors is contained in the oft-repeated question "Is it two or four at figure so and so?" or "Do you take it in two or four?" Quite a simple question, but very often difficult to answer. General rules hardly solve any problems, but at the risk of starting a mare's nest I would suggest the following guide.

When the beat seems to be too fast and exercises too little influence on the players, and the players could do *just as well* with less; or if fewer beats *do not create more difficulties* but in fact make the passage in question easier to grasp, then cut down the beats; or when the number of beats seems to *impede* the movement, cut down to half; or if you are beating for unimportant portions of the music again, cut down the beats. But the cutting down of beats must never be done at the expense of efficiency or from a wish to save oneself exertion. A musician must decide these questions for himself and not follow slavishly in the footsteps of others. Very often well-known conductors make mistakes of this kind and, either through lack of preparation or misreading of the mood of the music, beat four instead of two, or twelve instead of four or vice versa. Students should solve every problem from its musical point of view first and then work out the arm movements. Indeed this is the natural thing to do and hardly needs comment.

$\frac{12}{8}$ can be a real problem at times. It is so easy to drop into four beats in many $\frac{12}{8}$ movements and the excuse very often is that "these classics need brightening up". The trouble is that "these classics" are systematically ruined through this craze for fast tempi and some extremely beautiful movements are ruined by being taken too fast. Some conductors fondly imagine that human beings today think faster and are moved faster, and their emotions being quicker require in consequence that everything should be speeded up, but they forget that the beauty of many pastoral-like $\frac{6}{8}$s or $\frac{12}{8}$s disappears when taken too fast. If the conductor will concentrate on getting the utmost beauty out of slow movements—beauty of phrasing, of tone and nuances, then the public will listen willingly—the slower the better.

Some conductors may imagine that the music-lover only looks for speed ("the classics brightened up") whereas the real music-lover is *not* wholly impressed by a slick performance but wishes to hear the *beauty* and the *wonder* of some of these lovely melodies. If half the time were spent during rehearsal on tone, nuance, phrasing and ensemble instead of making the players "practise" passages which at the excess speed taken have become over-difficult, our concert halls would be more full then they are. Do not make the mistake of thinking that our forefathers had no feelings for beauty of tone and nuance. They *had*: they were much more in touch with humanity (they had more time), and without doubt knew and felt emotions very strongly. In that respect I am certain that the music of the so-called "classical period" was as important emotionally to the people of that period as modern music is to us. Not until the older music is made to live, through the sincere feeling and love of a conductor, will it receive its finest interpretation.

The conductor who seems to understand this more than any other is Toscanini, who makes the symphonies of Haydn and Mozart, and the compositions of Gluck and Rossini, sound very beautiful. Few, if any, nuances are actually written in the scores of these composers but they are inherent in the underlying spirit of the work.

I have wandered somewhat from my point and will continue the question of technique as applied to slow tempi. Interesting slow tempi to conduct are the slow, yet not too slow, $\frac{5}{8}$ and $\frac{7}{8}$. It very much depends on the character of the music as to how difficult these times are, but again it is when the tempo is just on the "borderland" of too fast for five and too slow for two, (one short and one long or vice versa) that doubts spring up in the mind. This doubt must be set at rest before the first rehearsal takes place. By that I don't mean that one must not alter one's ideas—but that it is not good to go to a rehearsal in any doubt as to what one is going to do until one tries it. Musically, however, the question of tempo should be firmly fixed in your mind. A lot may depend on the members of the orchestra. If the passage is really difficult you may have to help the players by beating more beats till they have the rhythm firmly impressed on their minds, after which revert back to the beat you had originally decided upon.

I give below a short list of slow pieces which will repay the student all the study he can put into them:

de Falla, *El amor Brujo* (the $\frac{7}{8}$ movement already referred to).

Bizet, *L'Arlesienne Suite, No. 1* ("Adagietto").

Beethoven, *Pastoral Symphony* (slow movement).

Beethoven, *Symphony No. 4* (slow movement, last few bars).

Beethoven *Eroica Symphony* ("Marche Funebrë").

Beethoven, *Symphony No. 1* (introduction 1st and 4th movements).

Debussy, *Iberia* (2nd movement).

Debussy, *L'Apres midi d'un Faune* (last two pages).

Franck, *Symphony in D minor* (introduction).

Haydn, *London Symphony* (introduction).

Mozart, *Prague Symphony* (introduction).

Wagner, *Tristan* (preludes to Acts I and III).

Wagner, *Mastersingers* (prelude to Act III).

CHAPTER VI

INDEFINITE PROBLEMS

INDEFINITE, yet very definitely of great importance. On the one hand, in conducting technique you have the problems of arm movement as applied to time-signature—a big enough study on its own—but we cannot pretend that this side of a conductor's technique is the most troublesome. There are the indefinite and unexplained problems of (1) "free" conducting, (2) pauses, and (3) cutting off—endings of note values—which trespass into the realm of interpretation, and a few words in explanation of some of these doubtful points should prove of use to the student.

(1) First of all let us deal with the problem of "free" conducting of "free" passages. There are a great number of examples illustrative of my meaning, but I will quote one or two only. In the Liszt *Rhapsody in D Minor*, the opening presents a real difficulty simply because in a sense it does not conform to any hard and fast rule of beating time. In other words it is free and must be dealt with in a free manner. Some arrangements of this work for orchestra are so altered that the rhapsodical nature of this Hungarian theme is easily conducted in the normal way. On the other hand there seems to be no known method of handling the free version of the original. It simply must be dealt with in a free manner and thus several more beats are added to the normal four in a bar, and the members of the orchestra must be told exactly what you are doing. In this particular case nearly every note of the tune should be "beaten out" to get the real effect. As far as possible no actual down beats should be used, but if possible three up beats (as in the last three of a $\frac{12}{8}$).

Another example is the first number of Dohnanyi's *Ruralia Hungarica* at figure 10, bars 2 and 3.

Here almost every note should be "beaten out" to get the intended effect and this can only be done by a series of short up beats. On the other hand it is possible so to rehearse the first violins in this passage that the players will do this without any special effort on your part at the performance. But this looks rather tame and is not altogether recommended—I discuss this point in a later chapter.

Another example of "free" conducting is the celebrated bars in Rimsky-Korsakov's symphonic suite *Scheherezade* (1st movement from letter F onwards).

In this example the strings must be started off on a rhythm of repeated pizzicato notes while the soloist plays a cadenza. This is not so difficult as at letter L and following bars. The only thing that can be done is for the conductor carefully to explain to the strings the exact speed of the pizzicato and to beat four slow beats in the "a tempo" bars. A very slight pulse beat should be kept up in the cadenza bars to assist perfect ensemble so long as it doesn't disturb the solo cadenzas.

There are other examples containing cadenza-like passages which must be controlled with a greater number than the normal beats in the given time-signature. An understanding with the players is all that is required to ensure smoothness in performance.

Very often it becomes necessary for an operatic conductor to conduct two or more singers on the stage in a cadenza passage while the orchestra must wait to be brought in with a final chord. Here the problem is a well-known one and no comment is necessary. It is a matter for conductor and orchestra at rehearsal. The players in any case use their ears and require no guidance beyond a definite beat at the appropriate moment. Another example which would repay study is the cadenza in Elgar's *Violin Concerto* (last movement).

(2) Most young conductors at some time or other are worried by pauses. The chief worry seems to be "Should I take the players off before continuing the movement?" or "Is a down beat continuing the movement all that is necessary?" It very much depends on the nature of the pause, of course, and as this destroys the possibility of making a general rule we will discuss some examples. Let me say first of all that I believe pauses should be looked upon as, in the main, startling holdups of the movement, dramatic in the extreme, and therefore there is bound to be a complete silence for a moment afterwards before continuing the movement. This therefore presupposes that

there should be a cut off, with another arm movement required to recommence the movement.

The quiet pauses in *pp* passages generally conform to this rule. I think the best example of a pause in which the student may feel doubt is the Beethoven *Symphony No. 5*, 1st movement, second and fifth bars. These pauses can be interpreted two ways—first with no pause of even a moment on the barline, and therefore no extra beat is required for a "take-off" (of the pause note) but only the down beat of the third bar. In the slight preparatory beat which one naturally gives before a down beat, actually what happens is that the players regard this as a sort of "take-off", or if they don't, they *use* the time occupied in the preparatory beat in preparing for the next bar, or maybe they use (in the case of the fifth bar) the rest at the beginning of the bar as a take-off. There are two questions involved here: (a) is it possible to get good ensemble in the quaver rest (all "take-off" together) when so many players have different ideas as to the value of a holding note (pause note)? and (b) is it the sort of pause demanded by the music?

In regard to (a) some players will hold on to the first pause note (the E♭) till the last moment; others will take their bow off the string in good time. On the other hand if the conductor gives no sign at all that he is going on without a "cut-off" the players will be compelled to hold on to the first pause as long as possible; but the trouble of this is that the rhythm of the three following quavers will in all likelihood suffer. Of course this can all be obviated by having an understanding that the players should "take-off" during the preparatory up beat, but these very fine points of orchestral ensemble are often left to the players and consequently some of the strength goes out of the playing. This brings us to (b): Is it the right kind of pause demanded by the music? This may or may not be an individual matter and it is useless to lay down hard and fast rules about it. On the other hand I feel I ought to give my own opinion as it may help to stimulate an enquiring turn of mind in the student.

Allegro con brio

For my part it seems as if even the *beginning* of the Fifth Symphony is a dramatic pause in the middle of some gigantic utterance. The mood is always upon me before I get to the point of commencing the work and it is (I speak personally) with the utmost difficulty I can raise my arm to give the necessary down beat for the first bar. Thus it is bound up with a feeling of awe and almost terror and certainly full of grim yet sublime drama. So I make a definite break after the second and longer pause. It is just as if one announced to a friend some grim fatality with a voice full of intensity, and after a short pause one begins to relate the event which led up to this tragedy. I don't pretend that this is my idea of what Beethoven tried to convey but it illustrates my point for the purpose I have in mind.

I think that the only *safe* rule to have on this point is (a) that when the pause *is* a dramatic one and a definite break in the continuity of thought, then there must be complete silence for a moment after; but (b) when the pause is only the preliminary to a greater pause, then a down beat (the next beat) should be sufficient so long as the players know what to expect.

Another example is Weber's *Oberon* Overture. It is evident that the pause at the end of the first bar has just that finality about it which makes a clean break necessary; so in this case also a "take-off" arm movement (or wrist movement, or any other movement sufficiently clear) is called for.

Adagio Sostenuto   Violins

Horn Solo

But a little later on at the end of the sixth bar one feels that the pause is momentary only and that no "take-off" is necessary. In fact at that moment a break in the continuity would

be a mistake and all that is required is that the conductor should give a down beat for the next bar.

This illustrates the difference quite clearly between the two kinds of pauses, and the student must decide from the musical point of view the nature of the pause. Having done so the following advice will be of help.

If it is a "complete break" pause, work out exactly the number of beats required and add the appropriate "cut-off" beat. For a tranquil movement—a turn of the wrist, or a caressing motion of the left hand, or a dropping of both arms quietly and slowly.

But for a dramatic pause, a big sweep, sometimes of the whole body following the right arm, will suffice.

Then there is the sweep of the baton across the body down to the left side, followed by a quiet dropping of the arm to its full length, bringing it back quietly to the "rest" or "commence" position.

The other kind of pause—a pause on the bar line when the whole bar is beaten out and when there are many notes still to be played during the last beat (semiquavers or demisemiquavers generally) the movement required is a complete drop of both arms at full length after the last beat. An example of this one will find in Strauss's *Tod und Verklärung* (page 51, full score); and again in the same composer's *Don Juan* at page 77, letter W. The *Don Juan* pause is most dramatic and requires a dramatic and big gesture in which the conductor seems to fling back the terrific sound at the players and immediately to drop his arms to his side, then raise them again quietly.

The difficulty of deciding what to do after a pause note, is one which is continually coming up during the course of a conducting career.

Often the tempo of the music is another factor. Frequently, although in slower tempi an extra arm movement will be necessary to "take off" before continuing the movement, in faster tempi the pause and the silence afterwards will be of such a short duration that *any* other movement except the next beat would be absolutely unnecessary. The effect intended would be of a very short silence after the pause and any extra movement would be out of place.

I hope I have said enough on this point to make it quite

clear. Of course the examples of the pause are legion and the subject is endless. There are other varieties, but technically they don't present any problems.

(3) I have in (2) dealt with the technique of the "cut-off" as applied to pauses. It needs very little further explanation except in one or two aspects. The arm or hand movement for the "take-off" (or "cut-off") will be invariably the same, but sometimes a "cut-off" is badly required in certain works where the length of a note is in doubt. Often the ending of a movement written in crotchets or dotted crotchets in a slow movement or a minim in a faster movement requires some little extra twist at the wrist to denote the cut-off. I am thinking of the end of the Brahms *Symphony No. 1* Allegretto movement. Here the note (a crotchet in a $\frac{6}{8}$) can be interpreted in two ways; either short, or at its correctly written length. Personally I think it is a legato chord and therefore requires such an extra twist of the wrist to bring the players off together.

Another example of this very indefinite point is contained in Haydn's "Spring" (*The Seasons*). At the end of the chorus "Come, Gentle Spring" there are three crotchets followed by quaver rests. A gentle "cut-off" movement is required here especially in the rehearsal period so as to ensure identical interpretation from all the choristers as to the length of the note.

In most of the examples, especially with a choir, an extra arm or wrist movement other than the beat is required to ensure correctness of detail and in most cases a twist of the wrist will be sufficient.

Chapter VII

USE OF LEFT HAND AND ARM

The Left Hand

Now we come to a really indefinite and obscure aspect of the conductor's technique. In regard to this point most text books will tell you that "the left hand is to be used very sparingly and when not in use is to be kept firmly at the side", or words to that effect. Yet I have always believed that the left arm and hand contribute much more to the success of a performance than the right.

The right hand is the time master; the left is something more—it is the director of phrasing, nuance, very often intense dynamics; and there is in most conductors a subconscious technique of the left hand, subconscious to such a degree that if you told them they *used* it, they wouldn't believe you. Some conductors, of course, have neither technique nor use for the left hand: it is either a pale reflection of the right or hangs limply by the side. Some just flap the left arm in time with the right—a boring and ugly habit.

First let me deal with the quieter moods of music in which the left hand can wield a great influence on the players.

Gradation of Tone

There is a movement—a hand movement—which controls gradation of tone (nuance) which is performed by a gentle turning of the palm upwards while moving the arm in the same direction. This implies a crescendo, and the opposite action diminuendo.

This is a stark description of a very graceful movement. As a matter of fact, the grace of the movement depends on the individual, but at the climax of the crescendo (a very gentle affair in any case) the hand opens out fully and with the arm outstretched and palm open to the players it quietly sinks down to below the waist. The latter action is almost like a reproof to

46

the players to be careful not to make an unsensitive or rough crescendo. It is like a large-hearted caress, and has, no doubt, the desired effect on the players.

This movement can be used in conjunction with the right arm for a much bigger crescendo and diminuendo. Then the two arms are almost a reflection of one another.

SOFTER; LOUDER

These two left-hand movements are seldom the same in the technique of conductors, but the most usual movements will be discussed here.

LESS TONE

To soften the tone, or to convey to the players that you wish them to play quietly—especially during a performance when the quantity of tone seems inexplicably louder than at the rehearsal—usually the left hand is raised on a level with the face, and brought down in an outward direction, palm outwards—to the side—making stops on the way.

MORE TONE

The movement used to convey a request for more tone can be done (and is usually) in two ways. First when it is just extra tone required in a phrase the left hand is raised from the down position, palm up, in exactly the opposite way to the "softer" movement. It is as if one were supplicating the players to assist in making more tone. Then there is the lightly clenched hand and fist shaken vigorously in the direction of the players concerned. This is for hard big tone and looks as if one were holding a heavy weight in the hand.

CLEARNESS OF DETAIL

There are other very delicate movements of the left hand which, although difficult to explain, yet play their part in the technique of conducting. I refer to a curious movement as if one were opening a shutter from the right side in front of the face with the thumb and two fingers of the left hand, the other fingers being fully outstretched. The meaning of this is not always distinguishable, but I always use it to denote absolute clearness of detail in regard to the playing of long phrases.

In any case the movement is such a delicate one that whatever the meaning intended—*so long as it is inherent in the phrase at the time*—it will convey enough to the players to make your meaning clear.

CRISP CUT-OFF

Then there is the delicate yet crisp cut-off frequently used by the left hand in scherzando and light passages. This is made by a swing around of the fingers from right to left describing a complete circle and at the end of it a sharp intake of the fingers as if you were clutching a handful of air. Sometimes this is used for light and crisp accents and is most expressive. Very often it is used to indicate to the percussion players the lightness required. It is worth practising.

PHRASING

Next there is the hand movement used to show your ideas as to phrasing and to denote these to the players. This is done by completely stopping the flowing movement of the hand and suddenly turning the downward palm to the right and continuing the movement suddenly in the opposite direction. This movement works out vice versa sometimes. The hand may be travelling to the right with the palm facing right and suddenly at the end of the phrase the movement is stopped, the hand turned as far in the opposite direction as possible and the arm made to travel in that direction also. It is extremely difficult to describe this movement and the student should ask for an illustration from his tutor.

There are many variants of the movements described but these variations occur in their proper place and are quite unconscious during performance.

LEFT ARM MOVEMENTS

Next we may deal with the left-arm movements which are used in more robust passages.

There is the swinging cut-off movement of the whole arm from left to right sweeping right across the body and finishing up sometimes in front of the face or falling down to the normal position. Sometimes this movement is specially called into play when the right hand is still beating time. This cut-off is used when the choir needs cutting off but the orchestra still plays on. The arms are used quite independently in this case.

Crisp Chords

There is the crisp chord which requires a short, sharp movement of the whole arm, as if one were throwing a ball at the players. The essential point is that the moment the arm has achieved its purpose it must rapidly swing to its normal or any immediately following position.

Crescendo molto and "fp" Crescendo

The quick crescendo is done with the same hand movement but more of the arm is called into play and the whole movement is rougher. In regard to this, there is also the brilliant *fp* crescendo to *ff* which one frequently comes across. Both hands and arms are used in this. The arms, immediately after the beat (the *fp*), sink down to as low a level as possible and, rising gradually (the right meanwhile beating a small beat if *necessary*), reach the limit of height, after which a strong "take-off" beat is given. The whole body can be brought into use in this movement. The gradual raising of the arms (and the body) illustrate very clearly the idea of a tremendous crescendo.

This movement should be used very sparingly and with the utmost finesse, otherwise it is apt to be misunderstood.

Rebounding Arm Movement

There are many other movements which can be very useful at times but which, if used too much, lose their meaning. One of these is the rebounding arm movement employed when a tremendously strong chord is struck or when you wish the players to give of their utmost strength.

This is a most effective movement and conveys its meaning instantaneously. The arm is brought down with tremendous force and *seems* to rebound several times with the force used. To the players this undoubtedly has a definite meaning. The conductor must take great care that he does not injure his arm muscles by too realistic a movement; there is no need to use more energy than for a normal beat if the movement is done in the right way. By that I do not mean that he has never to use his utmost energy—if he has the temperament of an artist he will be compelled to use it—but rather that the greatest care must be exercised to avoid injury to the muscles.

A list of the works mentioned during the course of Part I. Miniature scores can be procured for all these.

Overture *Portsmouth Point*. Walton. (O.U.P.)
Don Juan. Strauss. (Universal.)
Tod und Verklarung. Strauss. (Universal.)
Salome. Strauss. (Furstner.)
Overture *Rosamunde*. Schubert. (B. & H.)
La Mer. Debussy. (Durand.)
Overtures and Symphonies. Haydn and Mozart. (B. & H.)
Overture *Hansel and Gretel*. Humperdinck. (Schott.)
"Carillon", from *L'Arlesienne Suite*. Bizet. (B. & H.)
"Siegfried's Journey to the Rhine". Wagner. (B. & H.)
Symphony No. 4. Sibelius. (B. & H.)
Die Toten Insel. Rachmaninoff. (Guthiel.)
Ballet Music. *The Perfect Fool*. Holst. (Novello.)
Le Sacre du Printemps. Stravinsky. (Edition Russe.)
Rhapsody in D Minor. Liszt. (Eulenberg.)
Suite, *Rurulia Hungarica*. Dohnanyi. (Rozsavolgyi.)
Scheherezade. Rimsky-Korsakov. (Belaiaff.)
Violin Concerto. Elgar. (Novello.)
Symphony No. 5. Beethoven. (B. & H.)
Overture *Oberon*. Weber. (B. & H.)
Symphony No. 1. Brahms. (B. & H.)
The Seasons. Haydn. (Novello.)
Symphony No. 35. (Haffner) Mozart. (B. & H.)
L'Après-Midi d'un Faune. Debussy. (Durand.)
"Clock" Symphony. Haydn. (B. & H.)
Iberia. Debussy. (Durand.)

PART II

STYLE AND PERFORMANCE

Chapter VIII

ON STYLE IN CONDUCTING

I PROPOSE now to lay aside theory and to give the student some actual examples to study and practise, but what I have said in Part I must have been thoroughly mastered before the following difficult excerpts are attempted.

In an earlier chapter I left for further discussion the subject of control of oneself while conducting. I feel this subject is of supreme importance to students because it can make or mar the whole style of a conductor.

Too much has been made in the past of the conductor who in a magical way hardly moves his body, arms or head, and yet who produces amazing and lively performances. Toscanini has been quoted as the supreme example of the great conductor who hardly moves his arms and yet gets stupendous effects. Well, the first time I saw Toscanini conduct (he was then 65) he infused the utmost into his conducting—so much, that it seemed dangerous and most exhausting for his age. What he must have been like when he was young and full of youthful fire isn't so difficult to realise. Some friends of mine who saw his farewell performance in New York in 1931 told me that even then (he was suffering from arthritis) he threw his whole physique into his conducting.

Weingartner, one of the greatest conductors, says in his book on conducting (page 44, first paragraph): "Some conductors are reproached with making too many gestures—not without reason, for the mechanical element in conducting is by no means beautiful in itself and the black-coated figure with the baton-wielding arm can easily become ludicrous if the arm gesticulates wildly instead of leading the men, and the body also twist and curves in uncontrollable emotion. A pose of assumed quiet is, however, just as repellent."

Well, there it is. I think that every member of an audience has the normal amount of flesh and blood in his make-up and likes to *see* the conductor enjoying the more robust moments of music as well as the quieter ones. It must surely be something akin to an insult to see a conductor apparently unmoved during the performance of great music. I wonder what is the attitude of the orchestral artist? If asked he would probably say "He is at least sincere." An orchestral artist may not like to see an exhibition of temperament but it is a well-known fact that a temperamental conductor transmits his interpretation more successfully to an orchestral artist and gets a more musical performance as a result.

It is the excess of *movement* in the quieter moments which more often than not is not backed up by sound musicianship and which every good orchestral player fears.

An orchestral artist must be thrilled "out of himself" if success is to come to the conductor. To thrill a player *beyond* mere respect for your musicianship should be the aim of any conductor if he would be a success. Enjoyment is catching. If a conductor shows he is *enjoying* the mood of the music the players will without doubt *give* more, and the performance as a result will reach a very high standard. Music will become real and the audience will be moved and express its appreciation in an unmistakable manner.

Conductors who enjoy the exercise of beating time are a curse. I have seen most great conductors, and all of them without exception feel music keenly and conduct it as if they were doing it for the first time. To a conductor of this kind music is always a fresh experience; his movements and the extent of them are adjusted to the mood of the music at that particular moment. It is the lack of this "living in music" and the feeling of it which is such a curse in the interpretation of "classical music".

In an earlier chapter I made some strong remarks about "brightening up" the classics and pointed out how excess of speed indulged in by some conductors takes just that spiritual "something" from the music of the earlier periods. (Let us once and for all have done with the description "classical".) Some of the most perfect passages are hurried over as if they were a mistake on the composer's part and just groups of meaningless notes or blobs on paper. On the other hand, I have heard lovely passages of Händel, Haydn, Mozart, and Bach ruined by conductors who affect the "academic" point of view. Compositions of the great masters become "dead" in the hands of such men.

Rather than leave my attitude in regard to this question in any way vague I would like to give you as reasoned and clear a viewpoint as I can. It has long been my belief that the "classics" have been interpreted badly for many years. The notes were played, generally either too loudly or too softly, either too fast or too slow, according to the conductor. Phrases full of beauty have been glossed over—unliving—dead. No nuance or gradation of tone, nor "rise and fall", in a melody which, if written by a modern composer, would be copiously marked and played with *some* attempt at a musical rendering.

No! The classics must not be "felt"—just merely "played" loud or soft according to the few printed marks. Why? Surely Mozart was a human being who felt just as strongly about music as our moderns do! One has only to read his letters to realise how strongly he felt about everything and how vivid was his life. His music must have reflected his warm-hearted and tender nature. Yet we are content to label his music "classic" and put it into the category "to be played, *not* felt".

To illustrate my point I will tell you that I played over to a friend Toscanini's records of the "Haffner" Symphony by Mozart. The slow movement and minuet of this symphony as interpreted by Toscanini is living and tenderly beautiful music. My friend, a learned musician and fine conductor, was incensed at the "liberties" Toscanini had taken. Liberties! My heavens! Mozart himself surely conceived his work in no other way. But, apart from this, listen to the same work "interpreted" by the average conductor who "respects" the "classic" composer, and then you will understand my point.

Before I heard Toscanini I had the sense to put myself in the place of Mozart during the writing of one of his works, the beauty of which is undeniable. To Mozart the work was living. It vibrated with life. There could not be such a thing as a "classic" point of view. He was writing with his brain afire and caught up into that transcendental state, when Beauty opened her bosom to his urgent appeal. The state of mind during the birth of his sublime melodies—at the moment of realising them—is something only a composer can really experience. Read Mozart's letters and you will see what I mean. Yet one of a sensitive, sympathetic and artistic nature can approach very near to the holiness of those moments, and once having done so, all sense of "dry as dust" interpretation must fall away. Our players must be reawakened to the beauty of this music and so long as the "classic" interpreter point of view prevails among conductors those works will remain "dead".

Well now, how far should conductors go in interpreting these works? What are the missing points? What is the difference between the two points of view?

Firstly, it is largely a matter of sensitive and artistic feeling for what is truly beautiful. There may be different points of view about this, but that is the happiest thing about music—that there *can* be two slightly different (mainly in small points) interpretations as beautiful as each other. The differences between equally good interpretations are dependent upon many factors—one being that no two performances can ever be exactly alike. Again, the personnel of the orchestra may be different, and, lastly, no two conductors live at the same speed or pressure.

But apart from this, some of the older music needs editing, or, in other words, obvious omissions of phrasing marks, staccato marks, and nuances, must be put in. Most of the standard editions of the older music contain few staccato marks and are either marked *f* or *p*, and when one thinks of the pressure of work, and the number of major works the older composers turned out, is it any wonder that marks of expression were left out of the score *eventually published*? The composer generally superintended his own performances and got as much out of the players under him as possible, but he left no permanent record, to the musician of a later date, of his own ideas re nuance, phrasing, etc., or interpretation. So in fact one may well believe that the notes with general marks of expression only have come down to us. If, for example, one could only find Mozart's original parts, the question would, I presume, be decided once and for all.

It must be this fact which has prompted later composers to be very careful to leave their scores carefully marked. But modern composers sometimes leave little to the imagination.

This may be welcome to some people, but even in these cases a conductor very often must decide how to bring off the composer's own idea by sometimes altering his marks. On the other hand no work should be approached from this angle. The composer knows what he wants in dynamics, but in his haste doesn't always write his ideas correctly. Frequently one will see this sort of thing:

which more often means:

It is a fact that engravers will put in *a crescendo*, but within an inch of the correct place, and so generations of musicians will mistake the composer's intention.

Then composers will write the crescendo mark $<$ on the last bar of a page and, turning over, will write another (really the same one continued) which the engraver will copy literally. Thus we get two crescendos which are meaningless—the second cancels out the first, and it is doubtful if the composer means a Subito *p* and another crescendo. In most cases either it means a forgotten diminuendo or a long crescendo. An interesting example of this is on page 5, figure 2, in Debussy's *L'Après-Midi d'un Faune.*

p legerement et expressif

What does this mean? Is it a crescendo to a *mf* and then a *p* subito, followed by a crescendo and again a *p* subito with yet another crescendo?

I am inclined to think that Debussy probably meant;

I have retained the original phrasing or at least what passes for the original in the printed copy. I can't help thinking that Debussy meant;

I have quoted this example at some length because it shows clearly how difficult it is to take the engraver's work for granted (even Debussy has been careless in his note values as the semiquaver triplets in the $\frac{9}{8}$ bar are given as demisemiquaver triplets. It only shows how easy it is even for a master to make a mistake), and in this respect it is for the conductor to go through a work carefully and edit where necessary.

How easy for an engraver to think these phrasing marks; (Note the inexact position of the loops)

mean:

whereas it more than likely means:

The point to remember is that once the piece is printed, any chance (especially with an unknown work), of reprinting it correctly is remote and not worth the expense *at the time*.

All through *L'Après-Midi d'un Faune* there are glaring examples of meaningless signs, and the best thing to do is to buy a set of orchestral parts, edit them, and never use anyone else's. One problem particularly is pointed out. Look at page 12 (full score), figure 5, and read on to the fourth bar after 5. The horns are marked *f* (en dehors) and the violins piu *f* yet the central tune at the moment is the violin theme because it is the continuation of that which is played in the previous bar by the cor anglais and the clarinets marked definitely "tres en dehors" (Molto marcato). The markings in the fourth bar cancel one another out and by so doing make the composer's ideas very obscure. This is not an engraver's error—either it was indecision or carelessness on Debussy's part. A conductor who asks that the horns play "en dehors" and the violins "piu *f* " would be literally following the composer's markings. Personally I alter the markings slightly by marking a crescendo in the violins' part from the *f* in the third bar to a *ff* in the fourth, and mark the horns definitely *ff* so that this counter-phrase, although being heard distinctly, does not cover up the violin phrase. There are other ways of interpreting Debussy's intention at this point. It is largely a matter of personal taste. The other points I have referred to are matters requiring urgent attention because they are, as they stand, meaningless.

To go back to our original discussion on the "classic" works, I would like to dwell a little on the point already partly discussed, namely the lack of sufficient guidance from the composer as to his intentions. I have already mentioned Toscanini's interpretation of the "Haffner" Symphony (H.M.V. record, New York Philharmonic Orchestra). If you follow it closely with a full score you will see that Toscanini has done some very daring things, but somehow we feel that everything he has done, although not marked in the original, seems to be *inherent in the music itself*, as well as being in the best possible taste. One drinks in the pure beauty of the melodies with their perfectly balanced and natural nuances. But this is Toscanini's editing. The nuances are put there by him and the work *lives* once again. I have heard the same symphony interpreted by other conductors but it doesn't live and vibrate as when Toscanini conducts it. That is the bare truth of the matter, but there is much more behind it. Toscanini, the sincere and great artist he is, one can believe, gave this work a tremendous amount of thought beforehand and surely either rehearsed those nuances carefully or wrote them in the parts. That sort of performance cannot be brought off so perfectly *in performance alone* even with the finest orchestra.

To go further into the discussion, one must always faithfully interpret the composer's intentions—yes, but sometimes there is no fully expressed intention there. How often does one meet a perfectly senseless *f* in the middle of a *p* passage, and how often does one slavishly follow those *f*'s? Sometimes an *f*, sudden and very loud in the middle of a *p* section, like the slow movement of the "Surprise" Symphony by Haydn, is definitely correct, but when one meets *fp* in the middle of molto tranquillo passages it is all out of proportion. My rule for this is to consider the *fp* the older way of writing an accent, which should be interpreted according to the passage it occurs in. In a *p* passage it is a slight accent, but in a *f* passage a heavier one.

This is a minor point and is probably apparent to most conductors. But the practice of marking in nuances in the older composers' works must be undertaken with care. In one's enthusiasm to "re-edit" one is inclined to go too far. Let me consider the problem more closely.

In giving a sensitive, artistic and tasteful interpretation of a great work—say of Mozart—one must cut all thought of exaggerated, sickly and sentimental nuances. Accents put in for brilliant reasons in a brilliant finale may be pardonable, but put in purely as a stunt effect having no relation to the beauty or shape of the passage or phrase in question is most reprehensible. The following questions must always be asked:

"What does this phrase mean precisely?", "Is it simply a thing of beauty by itself or does it bear relationship to other sections?", "Is there an emotional climax somewhere in it?", "Played as it is written, does it leave something still to be desired?", "Has it too abrupt and meaningless an ending played as written?", "What is the emotional plan of the whole section or movement?", etc. etc. These are only a few of the possible questions one might ask oneself (it is impossible in a book of this nature to go into the subject in full). Then, when one has asked and found an answer to the appropriate question, comes the searching for and testing of the best means to express the passage perfectly. Absolute beauty must always be striven for—absolute beauty in construction, for every great melody or phrase has a perfect construction which can be pulled out of shape by senseless nuances.

Then very often an inner part is lost, if not underlined in a sensitive way. Then there are the special markings which are purely mechanical and which clarify the underlying thought running through the work. Sometimes the upper strings must be *slightly* marked down to enable the chief theme played by the celli and violas to be heard. That is a mechanical process, but very essential.

STACCATO

One of the chief omissions from the full scores of older music is the staccato mark. Too many times it is taken for granted that the missing dot over a note doesn't matter. The omission of the dot can turn an otherwise good performance into a sluggish one. The staccato gives that amount of variety in length of note which gives such a relief to the listener. Also one gets that piquancy, vivacity and lightness of execution which is the life and soul of certain passages. Half the trouble in this country is that we are playing music that was bred and born in the soul of another nation, taken for granted by the composer and his own people, and seldom or never marked in his copy in the way of staccato and other marks, and consequently missed by the orchestral player who only reads what he sees. He is not to be blamed at all. Neither is the composer, who probably never visualised that his works would be played by musicians completely out of touch with what was an everyday tradition in the composer's own day and country. Technical efficiency in a player does not always mean that he has musical knowledge of this sort or that he can see into the heart and soul of what he is playing. Too often the British orchestral player is blamed for a sluggish performance when an examination of his music will reveal staccato dots missing everywhere.

Even printed full scores in the same edition do not always agree with the orchestral parts. (It may be as well to warn the student: Don't go to a rehearsal of a "classic" work without at least seeing that your score agrees with the band parts.)

Now comes the important question: What should be my guide in editing these works as applied to staccato markings? One answer is good enough: In quick, brilliant passages where all the notes are marked with dots over them, even the unmarked notes (especially the final one) should also be played staccato.

NON LEGATO

Included in this question is the more misunderstood one of non legato. Players often ignore the value of this variation of note length. They keep their bows "on the string" far too much. I often wonder if the English school of fiddle playing isn't entirely a legato one. If staccato is taught it seems to be taught as a "stunt" and not as one of music's most common, yet effective, dynamic markings. But non legato has never been taught as an element in itself. To quite a number of players it is unknown and, consequently, when you ask for non legato you get staccato. If you didn't point out the difference you would get legato always.

(This is a general statement only. Of course there are players who do understand the nature of non legato and staccato.)

In regard to non legato (except in very fast passages where there is no time to take the bows off the strings to any extent) the rule should be that the bow should actually come off the string. Wind players should definitely separate the notes. This separation must not be done in the sharp staccato fashion. It is, in the main, a *gentle* separating of two notes, letting "air circulate between the notes". In staccato the movement is like a bouncing ball. Literally one note should bounce to the other. The extent of the bounce (and therefore the staccato) is regulated by the speed of the movement in question—although sometimes the mood of the music will require a "sharper" staccato that the speed demands. With the older composers, as a general rule, *there was only staccato*; not, as with moderns, dot (·) and dash ('). It is quite possible that the old notation for staccato (the dot) has changed into our modern non legato, and in searching for a modern equivalent of staccato, composers gradually began to use the dash (').

However this may be, when interpreting the older music, the difference between non legato (and the observance of it) and staccato must be shown.

PHRASING

It would not be for me to point out this elementary difference were it not for the fact that in "classic" works phrasing and non legato-staccato are so much part of the music itself. (Frequently, wind players will phrase over a bar-line when obviously the composer doesn't want that. It just shows an utter lack of sympathy with the very subtle phrasing of the older writers. Today we have a very limited outlook in regard to phrasing. The older composers understood the value of non legato endings of phrases and *used such a device very frequently*. Today we think that Haydn, Händel, Mozart, and Bach *didn't know* how to phrase their melodies. How preposterous! All these composers had more experience of players and were so much more in touch with their problems than any modern composers. It is the conductor's place to see that the phrasing of the older composers is in the main strictly adhered to.)

There is a fond belief among musicians, mainly orchestral players, who imagine that the older composers never wrote phrase marks *over* the bar-line, and that is why sometimes they phrase in such short phrases. Nothing is further from the truth, and if we take any work at random we can see how foolish is the notion.

Take for instance, the "Clock" Symphony by Haydn. Turn to the Minuetto and notice the overlapping phrase

marks all through. Then notice in particular the second
section of the Trio—how Haydn has phrased the flute solo
followed by the bassoon solo. Some flautists may want to play
this phrased with loops over the bar-line: notice, per contra,
the overlapping phrases in the first violin part leading to the
return of the Minuetto section.

As an example of what I mean in regard to non legato,
let us glance at the adagio introduction to the same symphony.

Most musicians will play the first four bars as one long phrase,
but it should be played and interpreted exactly as it is written
(especially at the climax of the crescendo), non legato, and
non legato to the pause. If this adagio opening is played *as
written*, a wealth of variety in interpretation is immediately
realised. The non legato becomes absolutely satisfying, especially
before the sforzandos are played, after the second pause. The
sf takes on its real meaning when all sound *ceases for a moment*
before the accent. It becomes a most gratifying sound, as if one
had, in a leisurely way, swung back one's arm for a friendly
thump on the back of an old friend.

Another point which never seems to me entirely satisfactory
is that many orchestral players, when staccato notes follow
immediately after the endings of phrases, play these notes too
long. A staccato note must have silence before as well as after
it, to be a true staccato.

Here is an example:

"Clock" symphony by Haydn.

Surely this should be interpreted as follows:

Otherwise the phrasing will not sound clean to the listener.

Here is another phrase frequently misinterpreted:

slow movement "Clock" symphony.

The first B♭ can be played in three ways: 1. Legato; 2. Non legato; 3. Staccato. 1. is wrong; 2 is correct, but 3 is more in keeping with the mood of the music at that point, and to clinch the argument you will notice in the next bar *there is no note on the first beat*. This shows Haydn's inner thought quite clearly. Another point is that the first B♭ is, of course, in reality the end of the previous scale passage.

So this theme should be played:

FAST TEMPI

This brings me to the point where I must give my long-held point of view on speed. There are many conductors and players who incessantly play quick movement too fast. There is an absolute limit to the speed at which a string player, for instance, can finger a passage, and, more important still, manipulate his bow in staccato or even non legato passages. Often one hears staccato passages taken at a speed which precludes all possibility of the bow ever coming off the string, so that instead of a staccato it is nothing more than non legato. The fundamental fallacy is that speed gives vivacity to the playing. Speed can *never* take the place of staccato in creating a feeling of vivacious rhythm. Excess of speed in staccato passages robs the music of *all* its meaning, as well as discomforting a player and dulling his sense of music.

A safe guide to the proper presentation of staccato passages is to remember that with the strings there must be sufficient time given (at the speed you decide upon) to allow the players

E

to bring their technique into play. The same applies to the wood-wind (?) except that fast staccato may be in some cases much more difficult.

The above point of view applies mainly to fast staccato passages and not to passages where speed is absolutely essential. Speed in its place is one of the conductor's best assets and very often the most essential aspect of a work—and the greater speed the better.

Mozart says: "They think . . . to impart and fire by that means [hurrying the time] but if there is no fire in the composition it will never get it by quick playing."

Chapter IX

CHOICE OF BEATS

There are some puzzling problems in modern music for the conductor in the way of choice of beats. Very often he is compelled to choose a beat which only helps a section of the players, leaving the others to carry on as best they may. First of all we will deal with the simple problem of alla breve or, "common time". This is again largely a personal matter, but we can argue at times that four beats (in $\frac{4}{4}$) may be as faulty technique in some passages as two beats are in others. The only rule to observe is to give the players as much assistance as necessary, but *don't over-assist* them. While observing this rule, one should also remember another one. Never beat when there is no need.

If, on the other hand, in some of the difficult passages you desire to beat four rather than risk inefficiency by beating two, do so. This is a point that can only be decided by a conductor knowing his orchestra. It is a common thing in $\frac{4}{4}$ time to feel a strong alla breve pulse and frequently conductors will beat four instead of two simply because the alla breve is not marked. Similarly one is continually coming across time-signatures of alla breve which must be beaten in four. In these cases, although academically both may be correct, the more comfortable both for conductor and player is the more correct. There is a curious repugnance on the part of conductors to beat anything but what is at first apparent in the time-signature. The rule to observe in all cases is to know the work in question musically and then give the most efficient beat to it.

The perfection of technique is the skeleton of the conductor's art and the flesh and blood may be likened to his musicianship and artistry. If his "flesh and blood" are not right, the framework of technique is of no use whatever. The possession of a perfect technique can land a conductor into as many inartistic blunders as the non-possession of it. There is no road to artistic and musicianly perfection through technique, but an artist and musician with perfect technique will always secure a finer performance than the same artistry without the technique. The student must live a full life of culture and study music's problems to the full, and in time he will come into his own.

CROSS RHYTHMS

Another problem is contained in the frequent cross time of three against two, or three against four. It is almost impossible to get perfect ensemble by cutting the beats down to half, especially when the tempo is slow. Players must get used to playing three notes against two beats (or vice versa). Normally, this does not present much difficulty unless the odd rhythm is divided up into a series of notes. This can cause trouble. The safest way to bring this off clearly without undue risk to the ensemble is to over-emphasise the first and third beats in the previous bar, and thus give the players of the odd rhythm a definite idea of their second strong beat.

A very good example of this point is contained in Debussy's *Iberia* (2nd movement). Here the beat is ♪=92 (four in a bar). As a matter of fact, the tendency is to take it slower than ♪=92, and at that speed a crochet beat (two in a bar) is too slow to keep the music moving along. Later, as the speed increases, it is possible to beat two. The easy way out is to beat two as much as possible, but the ensemble is bound to suffer if this is done. (I consider it is a crime for a conductor to allow the possibility of bad ensemble. He must never risk it by beating too few beats in a bar.)

The difficulty at the tenth bar facing the celli and double-basses can be solved satisfactorily by giving very strong first and third beats, but even this will not help a player with a weak sense of time values. This difficulty must not be left to chance, as it very often is. Some conductors pass this over as if they expected it to go right—in fact, close their ears to it. Good players will get over this difficulty fairly easily, but one must remember that an orchestra is only as strong as its weakest member.

At figure 38 the same difficulty occurs. How is it to be successfully solved? There is only one way, and that is by persistent rehearsal with the players concerned. First, rehearse it with four beats at the correct pace (a bit slower would be better), then gradually give up the second and fourth beats. Go back to the four beats and then try it with the full orchestra. By such persistent rehearsal you impress the pace of the melody and the players *play* it at that pace during the performance.

At 39 the same difficulty must be overcome, but by the time you have got to that point the piccolo and first horn will in all probability have solved it for themselves in the same manner. From 43 where the pace is a little faster it is possible to fall into two beats, so that the horn soloist has little difficulty. On the other hand, there is no necessity to beat two, and a slightly faster four should suffice. The horn player soon adjusts his theme to the length of each bar. At 46 the temptation is to go into two beats again. This is quite permissible if the $\frac{6}{8}$ figure played first of all by the two flutes is not unduly hurried and the ensemble does not suffer. On the other hand, at the eighth and ninth bars after 46 the violin and trumpet will appreciate two beats. But it is not necessary to go into two at 46 and six beats ($\flat=138$) is not too difficult for the violins to put up with at the eighth and ninth bars.

At 47 again two is better, but the third bar after six beats are essential. At the eighth bar after 48 four beats are essential so the second violins, violas and celli must adjust themselves to the prevailing beat. Two bars before 49 two beats are called for, but from the second bar after 49 six beats are essential from there to the end of that movement.

There is another solution to the whole problem, of course, and that is to beat two from 46 till the third bar after 47, when six must be beaten; four at 48; two beats two bars before 49, returning to six the second bar after 49. The only other doubtful point is at 52, when in my opinion the $\downarrow$ of the $\frac{3}{4}=$ the $\downarrow$. of the previous bar. Therefore quaver beats should be used at $\flat=80$ (*circa*).

The end of *Iberia* presents a small problem. Debussy has explicitly written at the $\frac{3}{8}$ "Tempo I ($\flat=176$)" which works out in performance only *slightly* lower than the quaver of the previous $\frac{2}{8}$, but the trombone glissando *should* be brought out with a grand flourish, yet the tempo should not be held back. The chief point to make is contained in the penultimate bar. Here the trombone glissando down should be clearly heard as the cross rhythm of two against three and the trombone should be exactly caught up with the side drum on the second dotted quaver, together making a brilliant crescendo onto the last bar.

There is difficulty enough here to test the powers of any conductor and one can just imagine Debussy's thoughts while writing it. It constitutes an amazing finish to a brilliant movement. To bring it off requires many excellent qualities on the part of the conductor, plus good players.

Another aspect of the question of choice of beat is the fast $\frac{3}{4}$. Frequently conductors will choose three instead of one or vice versa. It is a much vexed question and too often the easiest way is taken, consequently either hurrying the tempo or making it impossible for the conductor to have sufficient control over the players.

It is more easy to lay down a rule in regard to this point than any other. If the tempo is on the fast side and there is not any appreciable division of the crotchets one in the bar should be beaten without doubt. If on the other hand the crotchets are broken up and if the tempo is not too fast, three beats should invariably be given. (Generally this applies to $\frac{3}{4}$ passages which contain many semiquavers.)

There are exceptions to this rule in slow tempi where one is the only possible beat in $\frac{3}{4}$. This is usual where there is a similarity of rhythm in each bar. But nearly always the choice of one in a bar is a matter of tempo. There are many passages where, although three can be beaten, one in a bar should be beaten. Usually this is again a matter of rhythm and the length of notes.

The golden rule to judge the fitness of two or four beats in a bar of slow tempo is carefully to observe your own feelings and how they react to the slow two beat. If you feel a void, as it were, in the middle of each beat (or, more strictly, *between* each beat) then control is not strong enough and four beats will be better.

Remember that although two beats may be easier for you and the players, by beating two you may tend to think of the work in the wrong pulse beat and unconsciously hurry up the tempo, taking the "bloom" off the work.

Especially does this apply to "Parfums de la nuit" (*Iberia*) and although the quaver beat makes things difficult for some of the players it tends at the same time to keep the underlying mood of the work always clearly defined. I heard this work once done in four and six beats, all through, and although one feared for some of the players, it turned out to be a most satisfying performance.

CHAPTER X

ENSEMBLE IN UNUSUAL PASSAGES

PIZZICATO

Now we come to the question of ensemble in unusual passages. First let me deal with pizzicato. How often does one hear this sort of thing in a pizzicato chord:

when the chord should be *absolutely* together? In some orchestras and with some players ensemble has actually become accepted as an impossibility. Nothing could be more annoying to a conductor who is sensitive to such things. Yet one hears it on all sides.

The fault seems to be due mainly to anticipation on the part of the string players. Generally the finger of the player is already on the string and through sheer carelessness or lack of attention he plucks his string too soon. The string is plucked at the *top* of the beat instead of at the bottom of it. A conductor should rehearse pizzicato chords where necessary so that perfect ensemble may be gained. String players should be rehearsed to play to the moment of impact, *not round about it*. The pizzicato should be delayed *until the last moment*, and when the ensemble note is heard *and not before*, the string should be plucked. This is a case when mere beat hardly counts. It is almost impossible for a conductor to give a *perfectly exact* beat to the moment of impact. In this the players have to use a great deal of control. They must be trained to listen carefully and wait for the moment of impact. By moment of impact I mean the exact time-moment and *centre* of the beat. *Every player must feel this for himself,* and if he cannot, no conductor, even with the most perfect technique in the world, can teach him. The greatest care must be taken in this respect: never to pass bad ensemble in pizzicato passages or chords.

ATTACK

Another problem for a conductor is that curious lag in attacks after a rest. One could quote many examples of this point. After the eighth bar of Beethoven's No. 5, when the main subject is resumed by the second violins:

etc. Care must be taken in all passages of a similar nature that this does not happen:

In the last example the tempo is not taken up till the second bar of the "a tempo". All these and similar mistakes can be rectified by careful rehearsal, during which nothing should be passed which disturbs ensemble. This mistake is fairly understandable as the quick "a tempo" after the pause is too much for some weak minds.

But the following example shows sheer laziness:

How often does one hear the quaver (marked **x**) played too late by some players? In some places such a mistake would not be noticed, especially if covered up by the rest of the orchestra, but even then it is unpardonable. Lack of attention, carelessness and deficiency of character are responsible for such a devastating mistake. But a conductor who passes such carelessness at rehearsal is not worthy his profession.

Then there is the lag of the brass, which most conductors have at some time to contend with. These things should never be passed at rehearsal. *But,* care must be taken to find out if it is a mistake or the result of bad acoustics. Acoustics may have something to do with it, but more often it is lack of vitality from the brass. There is only one thing to do—insist on the brass players anticipating their entry *instead of breathing when they ought to be playing.* Again, the conductor *must insist* on perfect ensemble *at rehearsal.* I cannot give enough emphasis to that fundamental point.

Rehearsal

The conductor may feel the closest relationship during performance with his players, but such an intimacy is not always possible at rehearsal, for there he is the taskmaster and it is no good thinking he is getting anything out of the players at rehearsal if he is not. The conductor must gain his point and insist on the players giving a phrase, or the whole work, the *conductor's* interpretation. Even at the cost of unpleasantness the conductor must stop and correct carelessness and inattention to detail.

The players will respect you all the more as, in the long run, they themselves desire good performances. Furthermore, the players sometimes know little more than their own part and may be impatient at the amount of trouble you are taking. If you are insistent they will soon see what you are after and will in the end assist you in any way. But do not rely on that; your business is to get the utmost out of the music, and do not let anything or anyone deter you from that.

In rehearsal it should be your aim to gain a perfect ensemble and balance of the instruments. A great deal of the balance can be helped out by thoroughly marking your parts beforehand. This is essential, and will save a lot of trouble. As far as possible let there be no waste of time marking parts at rehearsal, although if it is necessary, see that it is properly done.

ENSEMBLE

Ensemble, the most fundamental aspect of orchestral playing should be striven for always. In much playing ensemble suffers by players regarding their solo passages as "ad libitum" parts. This is wrong. The soloist must be subservient to the ensemble of the whole orchestra. At the same time, a conductor should allow the soloist as much individual liberty as possible, but *never at the cost of ensemble.* This must be the iron rule—nothing must ever come before it—and the members of the orchestra must be made to realise it in an unmistakable manner, *even at the risk of unpleasantness.*

But I must add a strong warning. In your desire for perfect ensemble you must not cramp the artistic rendering of a passage—and there you will find yourself frequently caught between two stools; for on the one hand you may have a very difficult accompaniment, and on the other a melody or time variation. What must you do? First of all, you must decide whether the phrase in question *really* requires rubato (or any other variation of strict timing), and if so you must then ask yourself if it is possible to control the difficult accompaniment so as to fit everyone perfectly together. Once you decide it can be done, work at it and do it thoroughly. Nothing must be left to chance. That is what a rehearsal is for. Be careful with all these time-variation places that the effect is really artistic and is allowable.

Very often a composer will write "a piacere" or "ad libitum" in the most impossible places. If you come across a place of that kind, do not hesitate to mark it out of the band part and keep the player to your idea of tempo.

I remember once engaging a splendid bassoonist who had been a pianist and fancied his artistic powers very much. I had great trouble to explain to him that a solo marked as such in orchestral works did not mean "ad lib" in time value or tempo. Nothing would cure him—especially of leaving out certain tutti passages. So I decided to get a new bassoon part and carefully marked out all "solo" passages and substituted the word "tutti". In "tutti" passages I did the opposite and marked "solo". Consequently, he played his solos in time and his tutti passages were never again missing. Needless to say, the cure was not altogether permanent, but the player saw the justice of what I was driving at and turned out to be a very fine orchestral player.

At the time this seemed a very unusual and difficult undertaking, but it is what one must always do, and with the whole orchestra if necessary. An orchestral artist must be made to realise that although he has solo passages in a work he should be big enough to give every ounce of his mind to the composition. If on the other hand the conductor is not up to the mark, the reputation of the orchestra is to be considered above everything else.

Chapter XI

PERFORMANCE

WHAT constitutes a great performance?

I have used the word "great", but with such a tremendous subject one could be forgiven for using such words as "good", "fine", "adequate", etc.

"Adequate" is hardly worth discussion, for it means nothing beyond "competent performance". Something more is required.

One hears oft-repeated the phrase that such and such a conductor "brought out the composer's intentions" in a work. Such a statement is very loosely flung about by people who, if they only thought a little more clearly, would realise the absurdity of it. Who knows the composer's intentions—especially after a lapse of time? Isn't it possible that the composer changed his idea or intentions from day to day while he was composing the work? Who is to say what the composer intended?

No! There is no such thing as the composer's complete and unadulterated interpretation except in a performance conducted by or presided over by the composer, and then only if the composer is a good conductor and has the necessary technique to impress his thoughts on the players.

The more I think over this problem, the more I come to the conclusion that there is no *one* interpretation of any piece of music. The only standard whereby any performance can be judged is by its artistry and musicianship. What other standards can one go by? Fine musicianship will always keep a conductor from doing ridiculous things. In the stress of modern life a conductor is apt to accept engagements which ought to be refused. For one thing he might not be able to give the time to the preparation of works, once familiar, but now slightly forgotten. At the same time, he may be engaged in a series of concerts which is taking every ounce of his energy, both nervous and physical. Sometimes he will undertake a concert or operatic performance and may conduct it in a way the student would do well to avoid! "Nothing misleads us more than when a wise man does something stupid, since it is just this that we are apt to imitate in him." How true!

The student must always keep a tight hold on his musicianship and strive to keep his youthful freshness into his old age. This is one of the soundest principles in life. The only way to keep this youthful freshness is always to approach one's music with a feeling of awe. Many conductors are forced to work at too strong a pressure, and in so doing lose touch with this freshness. In too many performances one hears glaring examples of bad ensemble, bad phrasing from the strings and wood-wind—and a lag from the brass players. Sluggishness prevails in every department of the orchestra. There seems to be an entire lack of "point in rhythm"—a lack of staccato. In fact, it is much easier to answer the question: What is a *bad* performance?

Then what *does* constitute a great performance?

Such a performance must show no signs whatever of the above faults. But there must be much more than technical perfection. Let no conductor despise such perfection. The greatest conductor will suffer if all imperfections have not been cleaned up at rehearsal. Nothing must be left to chance. Every doubtful point must be cleared up and only then can the conductor be entirely free to exercise his artistry untrammelled; when the thought underlying the composition is clearly brought out (what Wagner called the "melos").

Then there is something indefinite which has nothing to do with technique or even artistry which exercises the utmost power over the players during a performance. Seldom is this power used at rehearsal but it is most apparent at the concert itself. This is the attribute which is born with us. If we haven't got it, no experience, no technique, no musicianship can help us. It is a sort of fiery zeal which transcends all technique, all difficulties and all conditions. I have known conductors whose technical powers were almost nil but who were fired by this intense belief in the music they believed in and who have given almost miraculous performances. In some of these cases, it was only in one particular work or the works of one particular composer that this miraculous quality showed itself. Often this same conductor's lack of technique would cause him to give a very poor performance of one of the other works in the same programme.

But the great conductor must have a most catholic taste and be able to bring out the beauty in the works of *all* great composers. An intense love for beautiful sounds is one of the mainsprings of this intensity. Further than this I would not like to go. Belief in the power of music to express the innermost feelings of human beings is also part of this intensity.

Chapter XII

ON THE CONDUCTING OF CONCERTOS

ALL THINGS considered, the conducting of concertos will give the young conductor much to think about. With a big symphony also in the programme and possibly another work, maybe new or at least unfamiliar, the concerto, be it ever so simple, will need careful thought. There are always danger spots, notably transition from the cadenza into the coda of the 1st movement; picking up the tempo after a swirling scale passage so that the pianist or other soloist coincides with the orchestra on his last note. If this coincidence of ensemble doesn't quite occur the resultant hiatus can seem like a year instead of a moment.

There is only one rule that can be followed in all these instances and that is the simple one of the conductor learning them thoroughly from memory, having played or sung the passage many times.

To take a simple example of this sort of thing we will examine the cadenza-like passage of Max Bruch's Violin Concerto, op. 26, beginning on page 31 of the full score. The previous passages are all easy to coincide with the orchestra but this one commencing with a downward scale and continuing to the bottom B♭ of the violin, begins to climb again in an allegro $\frac{4}{4}$ (four semiquavers to a beat) until the bar before F. The conductor will arrange with the orchestra not to beat until letter F, and the bar before he will have fixed firmly in his mind, and will lift his baton halfway through the bar and be ready for the down beat exactly as the soloist reaches his last note—top A♭.

There are numerous such places in almost every concerto, and although musically they are all different, the same principle of knowing from memory the notes in question can be applied to all. (See Beethoven's Pianoforte Concerto No.3 in C minor, 3rd movement (rondo); Grieg's Concerto in A

minor, 1st and 3rd movements; Rachmaninoff's *Concerto in C minor*, 2nd movement; and Tchaikovsky's *Concerto No. 1 in Bb*, 1st movement (end of cadenza).)

In the Schumann *Pianoforte Concerto in A minor* there are no difficulties of the above nature, but there is a bugbear of a difficulty for the conductor in the 3rd movement—the syncopated passage consisting of staccato chords in a most intriguing rhythm.

This could well have been written quite simply:

but it hasn't and there is only one way of conducting it, namely, one-in-a-bar beat and as steady as a rock. Personally I have never once had any difficulty with this but I have known conductors (using a very expressive phrase) "sweat blood" over it. Often difficulties assume fantastic proportions in the mind of a conductor and this is one of that kind. Orchestral players of even moderate experience know this passage quite well and look forward to it with some relish as a difficulty worth

F

overcoming. If the players are not "fussed" by a conductor, the rendering of the passage becomes natural and comparatively easy. But I want to warn the young conductor that this self-same passage has often been played incorrectly without anyone noticing it. The correct way curiously enough is in the version I have quoted above (second illustration) but too often this passage has deteriorated into too short a rest at the bars marked + and this must be guarded against. To split hairs when the passage is such a "nervy" one is a question for the conductor's own conscience, and I will leave it at that.

Quite a number of difficulties which the conductor may have to contend with are often not of his making.

CHAPTER XIII

THE CONDUCTING OF CHORAL WORKS

THE PROBLEMS of conducting in all its branches are very much alike and the conducting of choral works is no exception. The problem in choral conducting is rather a matter of methods of rehearsal, for the simple reason that most choral societies are founded on an amateur basis. The choristers of a choral society are only bound by a love of music to attend rehearsals, plus a pride in the achievements of their own choral society. These singers up and down the country exhibit great enthusiasm and a loyalty that is beyond praise. For these reasons alone if for no other the standard of "singing together" is very high indeed.

One 'of the most beautiful effects in the whole range of music is unaccompanied singing by either a male voice choir (such as one hears all over Wales) or a full choir such as the Glasgow Orpheus Choir and others. The range of expression, colour and dynamics attained by the best of these choirs is quite remarkable. It is an art in itself and the methods adopted to achieve these results spring from a natural and deep understanding of singing. As a rule the success of these choirs is mainly due to the work of the conductors: their enthusiasm, understanding and realisation of the beauties of choral singing are all transmitted to each member of their choirs and the result is a great tradition, handed down from one conductor to another. Lucky is the choir which has a succession of conductors of great sensitiveness and understanding of choral singing.

Of the many conductors who achieve this beauty of choral singing there are few who ever become known outside their own town or village and their achievement is the more remarkable in that most of them are self-taught. Their methods are unorthodox in the extreme yet their results are extraordinary. I remember adjudicating at a local eisteddfod in Wales where there were three male voice choirs competing in the final for the coveted Male Voice Prize. Each choir was over one hundred and fifty strong, and I remember the difficulty I had in trying to decide the winner. In fact two of the choirs had to be placed first as it was quite impossible to say which was the better of the two. The other choir was a very good second. These choirs all came from small villages nearby and the singers were all either tin-plate workers or miners. Their standard of choral singing, expression and ensemble were in their own way the equal of the musical standard in another medium achieved by a great professional orchestra.

Their methods of rehearsal are their own secret and when one remembers that hardly one of these men can read ordinary musical notation but learn everything from "tonic sol fah" copies, one is amazed still further at the results achieved.

Having paid my tribute to the great work done by conductors and choirs alike in these out-of-the-way places I do not intend to analyse their methods but rather to take a great and well-known choral work as a basis for discussing how a conductor will deal with the preparation of such a work for performance.

Let us therefore consider as completely as possible the chorus numbers in Händel's *Messiah*.

Händel was an operatic composer, and while in London was the centre of immense operatic activity. He broke himself financially in a useless struggle for ascendancy over his rivals. The exact historical details of this we needn't go into except to comment upon the fact that he made up his mind to give up this struggle and turned to a new medium of musical expression the outcome of which was a series of sacred works known as oratorios. The *Messiah* was first performed in Dublin with great success and later in London. Since then the *Messiah* has been and is still performed at least once a year by every choral society in Great Britain and possibly in most other countries as well where choral societies function. The choice of the *Messiah* for analysis should prove of interest to the young conductor who has at his disposal either a choral society or a large enough body of mixed voices to perform it.

In the preliminary rehearsals my method of teaching the choir was to take the women and men separately, and, if necessary—and it was often necessary—each section by themselves. It is no good while these sectional rehearsals are going on to have the other sections sitting about doing nothing. Frequently an assistant would take a section at the same time in another room sufficiently far away not to be heard. In this way rapid progress was made and therefore little waste of time. Before bringing the sections together the conductor should put the finishing touches with special regard to balance *as preconceived by him* in his study of the work. Each chorister should mark in his copy all dynamics or alterations for the sake of balance which the conductor has directed.

The coming together of the whole body for its first rehearsal is an exciting moment. The sectional rehearsals have whetted the musical appetite of each chorister and each one is waiting for this moment. The conductor may find some of his ideas of tonal balance not effective and will spend time putting this right. At the orchestral rehearsal (there's usually only enough money for one of these with the choir) tonal balance may have to be still further adjusted, but if the conductor's work in the preliminary rehearsals has been really sincere and untiring these last-moment adjustments will be reduced to a minimum.

There are all sorts of adjustments a conductor may have to make in order to build up the tone of one section of the choir, either because such section may be weaker than the others or because the balance as between orchestra and choir is inherently wrong. He may have to "double-up" the altos with the tenors in order to give greater strength to the latter. The same may be necessary with the basses and baritones. Few composers would object to such "doubling" so long as it was done with discretion.

For the purpose of analysing the *Messiah* choruses I have decided to use the Prout edition published by Novello's. I therefore recommend the conductor to read the Preface to this edition in the full score before going any further. Prout has been criticised by some musicians for certain alterations, mainly note values, but his study of the *Messiah* from Händel's own manuscript has been thorough and wonderfully penetrating and I for one accept most of his findings. There is only one of these I am doubtful about (in "Behold the Lamb of God") but we will discuss that when we come to it.

The Overture

There us a curious tradition that Händel didn't mean that in the grave section of the overture the semiquavers should be played as such. I can only think that some early choral conductor passed over these faults and others blindly followed them. At eight quaver beats in a bar ($\flat=120$) these semiquavers will sound quite long enough. I would like to warn the young conductor not to have too much respect for tradition if it offends his sense of musical values. In the repeat of the grave section it is customary to have it played p. Here again the conductor will please himself. I would advise him however to think out his own scheme of nuance, bearing in mind the natural rise and fall of harmonic tension in this section. It is not necessary, and in fact it is positively inartistic, to play this introduction with a solid block of f tone followed by the repeat being played p. Anyone could think of that!

The allegro moderato which follows is more brilliant played at $\flat=126$ than the tempo Prout has advised. Again, certain additions to the meagre allowance of nuances Händel has written are advisable and a study of the rise and fall of harmonic and melodic tension is worth while and will repay the young conductor a thousandfold.

No. 2, "Comfort ye"

Prout's tempo is too slow. It would be better to play this about $\flat=100$ or thereabouts. A rise and fall of melodic tension is quite natural in each phrase. At letter $\boxed{C}$ the recitative chords should be played exactly where Händel has written them, but the last two chords *must* come after the word "God" for obvious harmonic reasons.)

No. 4, Chorus "And the Glory . . ."

The altos because of the low register of their beginning phrase may need doubling with the tenors in some choirs and here also a crescendo is needed leading into the f of the sopranos, tenors and basses. The curious running together of the two syllables ". . .ry of" on one note is an Italian convention brought into his choral writing by Händel and I for one approve of it most wholeheartedly. Some of the earlier editors of the *Messiah* altered the notation here by writing an extra note but I don't think it worth while discussing the subject any further. The tenor entry on page 11 should be very strong, with again the crescendo to the top E. The full choir at letter A should sing these bars with full voice. At letter B the basses and tenors on the words "for the mouth of the Lord", etc. should give full masculine tension to these notes. The soprano repetition on page 13 should also be sung with great brilliancy. For the rest of this chorus the above remarks should be followed. The adagio ending should be given with full voice and with the utmost legato.

No. 7, Chorus "And He shall Purify"

The soprano entry should be sung as indicated *mf*. The top Gs should be sung non legato and each first note of the semi-quavers would be improved by a slight accent, and the quaver before "the sons of Levi" must be staccato in order to give clear definition and a breath to the ending of the scale passage. This rule should be followed as each similar phrase is sung by the other sections of the choir. At the bottom of page 23 the notes in the counterpoint given to the altos should be strongly accented. The rendition of the scale passages in this chorus, and indeed all through the *Messiah* wherever similar passages occur, should be rehearsed in such a way *that each note is clearly heard*. The vowel sound of ". . .fy" in the word "purify" must be retained all through. The clarity of this and all other similar passages is a matter of vocal training where both the tongue and the jaw of each singer comes into play. I recommend that the ending of this chorus should be "a tempo".

No. 9, Air and Chorus "O Thou that Tellest . . ."

The tempo marking is excellent here. Each entry of each section in the chorus should be distinct. Care must be taken with the note values of "arise".

More often than not these notes degenerate into a triplet of semiquavers which is wrong and an example of untidy musicianship. I recommend at the bottom of page 40 a diminuendo in the last two bars commencing the final phrase of "the Glory of the Lord" *pp*, building up in the four bars to a *ff*. The orchestral parts should be marked accordingly.

No. 12, Chorus "For unto us a child is born"

I have heard this chorus sung in a uniform *ff* right from the beginning. What desecration! The wonder and beauty of the chorus is completely destroyed by such carelessness. Händel has marked each entry *p*.

During the long scale passages I have always divided the singers of each section so that there is no breath strain and no break in the continuity of the passage. This is effected as follows:

SUB
SECTION
A

SUB
SECTION
B

The climax of tone from the *mf* on the second line of page 49 with the addition of each section of the choir making a crescendo to the outburst of *ff* on the word "wonderful" is an notable example of Händel's intense feeling while composing this work. The dynamics in this chorus must be observed if Händel's intention is to make itself felt.

We come once again to the long scale passage but this time sung *f* by the sopranos and altos. Here it will be a wise precaution to arrange for a breath to be "snatched" by each sub-section halfway through the passage, but at different places. On no account can the sopranos and altos be divided into sub-sections this time as the full weight of tone is required all through.

No. 17, Chorus "Glory to God"

This wonderful chorus has something in it of unearthly beauty. The opening phrase for sopranos, contraltos and tenors is so well distributed among these voices (with the tenors going up to their high G in the third bar) that the sound produced, even by a moderately good choir, is of the freshest quality. The orchestration also helps to give a sensation of light and air. Händel has marked this phrase *mp* and the following "and peace on earth" *mf*. This should be observed with great care. Care also should always be taken with the endings of words and the "d" in the word "God" should be clearly enunciated.

No. 21, Chorus "His Yoke is easy . . ."

The orchestral accompaniment to this chorus should be kept down to the marking at the beginning so that each entry is allowed its full measure of *p*. The basses and cellos should play their quavers non legato so that the whole effect will sound light and "airy". It would be as well also that the sudden changes on page 76 to *f* and back again to *p* should be corrected in accordance with the voice parts. The *f* of the orchestra in each case must lessen (diminuendo) to the *p* in order that the *p* entry of the voices should be clearly heard.

The last phrase of all, "and His burthen is light" can be taken poco allargando.

Part II

This brings us to the end of Part I and from now onwards (in Part II) Händel reaches the highest point in expression and the meaning of words through choral writing that was ever reached by a composer. The drama and tragedy of the crucifixion is mirrored in the extraordinary beauty and mood of each chorus. The words give the clue to the interpretation of each chorus. The pity of "Behold the Lamb" is followed by the anguish of "Surely". The more hopeful mood of "and with His stripes we are healèd" is followed by the anger of "All we like sheep". Then a different mood sets in with the scornful nature of "He trusted in God". The prayer and questioning of "Lift up your heads" is answered by the certainty of "He is the King of Glory". The solo "Why do the Nations" is followed by "Let us break their bonds asunder". Again a solo, "He shall smite them" carries us forward to the thunderous chorus of jubilation, "Hallelujah". The crescendo of intensity from "Behold the Lamb of God" to the "Hallelujah" chorus is overwhelming in its effect on an audience and the young conductor will do well to so arrange his dynamic scheme with this end in view.

No. 22, Chorus "Behold the Lamb of God"

Controversy has raged over Prout's insistence on Händel's notation of the first syllable of "Behold" as to whether it should be a semiquaver or a quaver in length. Some editions give the length of this syllable as a quaver and I have never been able to make up my mind, not as to which is correct, but rather which is the most comfortable to sing. After changing my mind several times (in private) I have come to the conclusion that Prout's insistence was correct. If the tempo is correct the semiquaver will carry enough weight to be effective ($\flat$=80).

The very first entry (of the altos) should set the whole mood of the chorus. On each phrase I allowed a slight crescendo and diminuendo, but if there should be a tendency to exaggerate this I would rather dispense with this nuance. The bass entry in the second bar of page 81 should be very strongly marked. Again I would suggest some additional nuances starting "that taketh away" on the second line of the same page *mp*, making a molto crescendo to a *ff* the last bar of the same line. Immediately at B bring the tone down to *p*. At the third bar of letter B the sopranos should keep to *mp* but the altos, tenors and basses should sing *mf*, and the basses, particularly, should be well marked. On page 82 the basses should reach full tone in the second line and from the third bar the whole choir should soften gradually, finishing as quietly as at the beginning.

No. 24, Chorus "Surely He hath borne our griefs"

Prout's tempo $\flat$=72 is excellent. The orchestral accompaniment must never waver in its rhythm from beginning to end with the demisemiquavers played the correct length.

Many times in this chorus the conductor will have to make up his mind as to the *practical* length of certain notes so as to enable the choristers to fill their lungs. Both wind players and singers tend to breathe in the wrong place if the composer hasn't actually written rests for this purpose. The rule *must* be, for obvious reasons, that if any note has to be shortened for the purpose of taking a breath it *must* be the end-note of the earlier phrase, namely:

He hath borne   our grief,   and car-ried our sor-rows

Händel's manuscript is as follows:

The above remark may seem very obvious to the young conductor. I quite agree!

The only addition to Händel's markings which I allowed myself was from Ⓐ onwards. (The phrase "He was wounded..." I insisted on a slight crescendo to the word "our" after which a quick diminuendo. On the next phrase "He was bruisèd..." especially on its immediate repetition each note was accented and sung with a great intensity. These additions to Händel's dynamics are, to my mind, what every chorister feels when actually singing the words: furthermore they heighten the intensity of the passage.

The only other alteration (not an addition) was the slight quietening down of tone on the last phrase (orchestrally as well) after which the orchestra returned to full power.

No. 25, CHORUS "AND WITH HIS STRIPES . . ."

One of the main things the conductor has got to guard against in the performance of Part II is the comparative meagreness of the original nuances. The audience must have relief from the continual shattering *ff*, and, unless this is done by the time the "Hallelujah" is sung (the very time when the maximum tone is needed) the audience will have had enough.

In this chorus (much more hopeful in feeling than "Surely") the opportunity presents itself to bring down the quantity of tone as a "breathing place", as it were, before the next full-blooded chorus "All we like sheep". So I have marked down the *mf* at the beginning to *p* with an accent on the word

"stripes" and a crescendo-diminuendo on "we are healèd".
This I have done in the soprano and alto leads, but when the
tenors enter with the same phrase at letter [A] and the basses
at the bottom of page 91 because of the balance of tone and the
advisability of bringing these parts out, I have adhered to the
markings in the score. Gradually more tone is added and the
soprano lead on page 92 is given out with an expressive *f*. At
letter [C] the basses should sing full power. Care having been
taken in bringing out each "lead", the last line would improve
by being sung diminuendo to the end of the chorus.

No 26, CHORUS "ALL WE LIKE SHEEP . . ."

In this chorus I have always felt that an inner voice had said
"Now ye hath seen the error of thy ways" and the choir
angrily retorts "All we like sheep hath gone astray". Anger
is the keynote of this chorus so that there should be no suggestion
in it of a languid legato. A true non legato would be present
all through and the utmost brilliancy given to the scale passages.
The tempo marking ♩=92 is good. The dynamics at the adagio
should be observed carefully. Care again should be taken with
the sound of the "s" at the end of the word "us" and this word
should not be slurred into the last word "all".

No. 28, CHORUS "HE TRUSTED IN GOD . . ."

Again the mood changes and the fickle people rebuke the
Lord. ("He looked for some to have pity in Him, but there
was no man . . . to comfort Him.")
The tone used by the choir in this chorus should be harsh
and bitter, snarling out their words like a pack of wolves at a
kill. Again a non legato rendering is essential with hard accents
on the words "He" and "Him" with a strident crescendo on
the words "let Him deliver Him" and "if He delight in Him".
The tenor entry on page 106 must be heard clearly and should
be delivered with a tantalizing and sarcastic tone, the other
parts being brought down somewhat (but not the next bass
entry which should burst forth with fury).
At the bottom of page 106 I have scaled down the markings
a trifle so that again the tenor entry (sung *mf*) should be heard
above the others. Care must be taken all through with the

three words "delight in Him" so that the "t" doesn't run into
the word "in".

In the last bar before the adagio I used to make a rallentando
holding on to the word "Him" for a trifle longer than necessary
(but not a pause!) with a dramatic "take-off" on the down
beat of the adagio finishing as marked, *ff*.

No. 33, CHORUS "LIFT UP YOUR HEADS . . ."

Prout's insistence on Händel's manuscript is interesting here
as the phrase "Who is this the King of Glory" must be decided
upon one way or the other. Händel's manuscript gives "this"
and not "the". "This" is a more awkward word to sing on a
semiquaver at the tempo required ($\rfloor=76$—to my way of
thinking, a bit slow). Care is essential for the clear enunciation
of the two words "lift up". (They can sound too much "lif—
tup".)

After the *mf* commencement I advise a crescendo to "and
the King of Glory shall come in" which should be sung marcato.

The wonderful effect of the women of the chorus singing the
opening phrases followed by the questioning of the men is a
supreme example of the simplicity with which great composers
adorn their works. On page 117, after the quiet *mf* of "The
Lord strong and mighty", a crescendo should be made on the
repetition of this phrase especially on the words "mighty in
battle".

(There is so much that can be said about this chorus that it
really needs a chapter all to itself.)

Suffice to say that the general plan of dynamics (particularly
in the reiteration of each phrase) should be a general building
up of tone. In the tutti at letter [C] each part is responsible in
its own way in building up a solid block of tone but at the
third bar of letter [E] it would be well to drop the tone down to
p, building up the tone to *ff* the third bar of page 122. A
similar suggestion is made at letter [F] but in this case the
phrase should commence *mf* reaching in a crescendo the utmost amount of tone possible, especially in the last three bars.

No. 37, CHORUS "THE LORD GAVE THE WORD"

I have always regarded this chorus as an interlude, its chief
interest chorally is the magnificent opening for the tenors and

basses "The Lord gave the Word". Here the attack must be
both exact and strong. The conductor can use his fourth beat
as a take-off for the "d" of "Lord"—such a beat is essential to
get exact ensemble.

No. 39, CHORUS "THEIR SOUND HAS GONE OUT"

This is a chorus of jubilation. At letter [A] the magnificent
tenor phrase can be made still more effective in the following
way:

This marking gives each subsequent entry of this phrase a
chance to come through quite effectively.

At the end, the second bar of the last line on page 132,
there must be a "take-off" beat (the second beat) and the
tenor quavers on the words "unto the ends" should be accented very strongly. Again the second beat in the penultimate
bar can be used for the clear enunciation of "ends" before
the following word "of". (I note that on the top of the page
of this chorus in my own copy, I had written "To sound like
trumpets and trombones playing to the four corners of the
earth". A good description of the mood required.)

No. 41, CHORUS "LET US BREAK THEIR BONDS ASUNDER"

After the solo "Why do the nations so furiously rage" we
have the tremendously dramatic outcry at the futility of war.
The tenors must sing this with great accents and staccato.
Not only the tenors but each section as it sings this remarkable
phrase must treat it similarly. At letter [C] again the tenors
start off with a second subject treated fugally by Händel. The
identical interpretation is required as each section enters.
On the "(a) way" the tied note should be accented and full
length given to it. It will help the choristers if the first note of
each group of semiquavers has an accent. At letter [D] the
utmost vocal vigour should be used at each entry. Care must
be taken with the penultimate bar in the management of the
tenor part. An upward swing (extra to the third beat) from the

conductor will, with an explanation to the whole choir at rehearsal, solve this difficulty.

No. 44, Chorus "Hallelujah"

The tenor aria before the "Hallelujah" chorus is a mighty example of Händel's genius, and in the accompaniment a most exciting quality of brilliance in the playing of the violins will suffice to give just that intensity required.

Of the "Hallelujah" chorus itself there is little to say, for everything necessary for a brilliant performance is actually written down. Perhaps at letter B and similar places during the phrase "for the Lord God omnipotent reigneth" all the "Hallelujahs" in other parts should be scaled down a trifle.

One other suggestion I have to make is that the long holding note on the word "kings" should commence as a *fp* and crescendo up to a *f*. Particularly should this be so on the second line of page 154 when the sopranos have their rising phrases leading to the greatest climax of all at letter F. The last "Hallelujah" of all should be sung allargando.

Part III

No. 46, Chorus "Since by Man came Death"

The nuances I would recommend here are a *pp* beginning with a sudden sforzato piano subito on the word "death". The next phrase again commencing *pp* with a slight crescendo *in the soprano part only* to the word "death" and then diminuendo. After the intervening Allegro there is a similar passage at letter B which should be treated with the same nuances as was the first phrase.

No. 53, Chorus "Worthy is the Lamb" (and the final Amen)

The tempo marking $\text{♩}=60$ is very good for the Largo but I have always thought the following Andante ($\text{♪}=120$) a trifle too slow. A quaver beat is too finicky and I recommend a crotchet beat about $\text{♩}=76$ as being more effective.

The Larghetto that follows is marked $\text{♩}=72$ by Prout but even this I feel is on the slow side. These tempi the young conductor must decide for himself and his musical sense will be his guide. Each entry of the theme (first by the tenors and basses) is improved in its effectiveness by the addition of a crescendo up to the top note with a corresponding diminuendo down (not to less than f) but with the final "and unto the Lamb" accented. In fact the rise and fall of most of the phrases in this chorus can be treated in the same way. Care must always be taken that there is no exaggeration, otherwise the effect would be unmusical and somewhat inartistic.

It would not be out of place here if I added a personal note in regard to the additional nuances I have suggested all through this short dissertation on the rehearsing and conducting of the *Messiah*.

The first apology I must make is that it would have required another book with innumerable musical quotations to go more thoroughly into the question than I have done. The second apology is that I only offer these suggestions as a guide and not as directions.

When I first conducted the *Messiah* many years ago, and subsequently, for ten years, at least once a year, I was immensely affected by the tremendous virility of the work as well as by the dramatic intensity of it, particularly Part II. The meagre allowance of nuances seemed to me then, as it does now to some extent, to lead to a "dry as dust" approach to this great and noble work. With all the fire and enthusiasm of youth I set to to heighten, to clarify the enunciation, not only of the words, but the natural rise and fall of the harmony and the melodic line. I wasn't concerned with a startling interpretation, or a quickening up of tempo. Such things to my mind smacked of charlatanism. What I wanted was to bring out the meaning of the words, to heighten the effect of the wonderful themes and phrases, to build up the *intensity* of the drama until the jubilation of "Hallelujah" would be irresistible. In this way I evolved a scheme of dynamic in which this desire of mine became a practical possibility. At first I found many old choristers, who had been singing the notes for years without understanding what they were singing about, were rebellious, but by force of musical persuasion I was enabled to bring them with me. The result was a *Messiah* with an inner intensity of meaning which the public at once realised was *authentic*.

In the writing of music, expression marks are *not* the last word. Any composer will tell you how difficult it is to convey his meaning exactly. Composers will also tell you that musicians frequently misunderstand their intentions. Wagner gave up writing metronome tempi in his later works for the reason that even this fairly exact guide was so frequently misunderstood. Mozart, Händel and Bach in all likelihood superintended the first performances of their own work and directed the players in the manner and style of performance. Possibly the required nuances were added to the original orchestral and vocal parts. These are now lost and the composer's own manuscripts were published with the few indications left to us.

What are we to do? When the composer has written *ff* and little else for pages and pages and then a *p* for bars and bars, do we leave it at that?

When a composer in a choral work has written a *f* in every part as a general reading, yet we know that if every part was sung *f*, the principal theme would be covered by the other parts, what is expected of us?

There is only one answer: a careful editing after a deep study of the inner meaning of the work must be undertaken. But this must be undertaken in a deeply reverent mood, and if this is the approach, much can be forgiven and much will be admired.

So these additional nuances are only offered to the young conductor as a guide and must not be taken without serious contemplation as to their value and effectiveness.

Lastly, I have only dealt with the choruses. Space does not permit of a full analysis. As I have said above, a complete discussion of the *Messiah* is not possible in a book of this nature.

NOTE RE SEATING OF CHOIR

The arrangement and seating of a choir at performance has often struck me as being left far too much to tradition and the "look of the thing", rather than what is best for balance. The usual method is for the sopranos and contraltos to fill the forefront of the platform with the tenors and basses behind. For purposes of balance such arrangement is not by any means the best that can be done. There is no reason that I can think of why the question of balance should not be the chief

G

reason for the placing of the choir, and if this is so, the usual method as described above can only lead to inequalities of balance in performance.

I therefore suggest another arrangement as follows: facing the audience the sopranos should sit on the extreme left filling the space from the front of the choir seats, occupying one fourth of the front row, and extending in a block to the back. Next to them the tenors should be arranged likewise: then the altos, and lastly, on the extreme right, the basses. In this way each group will have at least *some* of their section in the front and the sound of the choir will blend to a fuller extent. Again each section will be more directly under the control of the conductor.

I advise the young conductor to experiment with this formation. He may think it better to have the sopranos and contraltos side by side, likewise the tenors and basses. Whatever the result of his experimenting may be, I still think any variation of the above suggestion better than the usual formation.

PLAN OF CHOIR SEATING

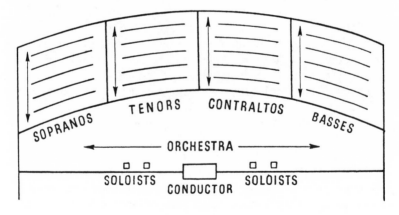

PART III
OPERA

HOW AN OPERA HOUSE EXECUTIVE FUNCTIONS

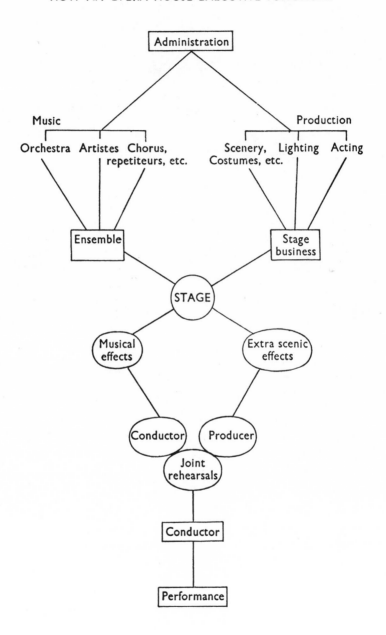

Chapter XIV

CONDUCTING AND REHEARSING OPERA

Before dealing with actual examples of operatic conducting it would be profitable to describe in detail the organisation and routine of an opera house. It is as well that I do this so that the young conductor should get a clear idea of the immense amount of co-ordination required in producing an operatic performance.

Opera is the fusion of five arts into a composite whole. Music, acting, singing, scenery, lighting are welded into one art,[1] opera, an art variously described according to the taste and mentality of the person as "that bastard conglomeration of arts" or simply the "art of opera". In regard to the former I can only retaliate by pointing out that "bastards" have often been most interesting and strong-minded mortals who have achieved great success in difficult circumstances and survived criticism most successfully. Be this as it may, opera has come to stay and, furthermore, has called forth the greatest efforts from even the great symphonists and "classical" composers. Another notable fact is that the great conductors have all learnt their art in the opera house where every difficult problem in conducting is encountered and must be overcome.

Musical Organisation of an Opera House

We will presume for the sake of clarity that our conductor has been entrusted with the task of building up the vast musical organisation required in order that the perfect performance of opera should take place. We will start with the essentials.

Repetiteurs. The first task is to choose at least six pianists who will be entrusted with the work of teaching singers their rôles. This looks quite easy. All you need is six good pianists!

---

[1] One must not forget the part played by ballet in opera, but as this is incidental in most operas and absent from some it cannot be said that it is an integral part of it.

But there's more to it than just this. The six pianists have to be much more than "players of the piano". Care must be taken that each one of these six corner-stone men should be imbued with a great enthusiasm for opera. Each one should know a great deal about the singer's art, and show great understanding with the aims and ambitions of singers; each one should know how to deal successfully with their many foibles and bring the best out of them: to be hard and adamant on the right occasions: to be sympathetic and helpful when required.

But further, each one of these men should know the type of rôle he is teaching. He should be able to build up in the mind of the singer, while teaching him the notes, a clear idea of the character the singer is about to portray. Mere teaching of notes is only half the work. So that a repetiteur's work is many-sided.

During the course of coaching a singer, a daily report should be made out giving the progress or otherwise of the singer. Such reports should be in the hands of the conductor concerned before the weekly meeting, so that the progress of rehearsals can be gauged. If a singer is a slow study it will be seen, and adjustments in the rehearsal sheet for the following week will be made so that the slow study can be kept in line with the quicker ones. It is the duty of repetiteurs to keep a clear idea in their minds of the time factor, and to see there is no waste of time; to report on the state of the singer's voice as to whether he or she is being overworked and therefore being overstrained.

I regard the work of the repetiteurs as being of the utmost importance and would go so far as to say that the whole success of opera is dependent on the sincerity and value of their work.

Here are a few rules for repetiteurs and a summary of their work.

Coaching singers:

(a) Never pass the slightest mistake, be it seemingly the smallest.

(b) Teach your singer the part as the composer wrote it.

(c) Make singers respect the true values of notes in recitatives.

(d) Don't allow a singer to put his or her own "idea" before that clearly written down by the composer. Leave that decision to the conductor.

(*e*) Never pass a section till the singer has sung it to you without his copy. That is the time to go on to the next section and so on. Correct all faults in intonation.

(*f*) Don't allow singers to sing half voice or an octave lower when learning a rôle. That can come later after the part is fully "in the voice".

(*g*) Never allow a singer to think a part is easy and therefore calls are unnecessary. You yourself must not be hoodwinked even if the singer might tend to be.

Apart from coaching singers, the repetiteurs have many other duties which can be summarised as follows:

(*a*) Taking the "beat" through a "peephole" in the scenery for off-stage music. Much can be said about this. A repetiteur must learn to recognise and understand the conductor's individual style. To anticipate the conductor's beat, however slightly, because of the "lag" of sound in some opera houses. He should never let his eye wander during the transference of beats. For this purpose the repetiteur *should memorise all off-stage music.* This is essential for many reasons. A stage-hand may quite inadvertently pull out his lighting switch. If there is a stage entry exactly where the repetiteur is standing someone might easily knock his score from off its stand.

A red or blue-coloured torch should be held in the hand of the repetiteur so that those taking part in off-stage music can see his beat clearly.

(*b*) The playing of bells. This is an art in itself. I recommend that each repetiteur should have a lesson from the orchestral percussion player before attempting to play bells.

A bell, particularly a tubular, can sound like a tin can if hit in the wrong place. The performance of that masterpiece of bell ringing in Puccini's *Tosca* (Act III) can easily be marred if one player (of the six) thinks bell-playing is beneath him. All behind-scenery effects must be performed with the utmost realism and in the true atmosphere required. One of the most beautiful and magical effects in the whole repertoire of off-stage bell sounds is toward the end of the "Pimen" scene in *Boris Godounov*, when the chapel bell intones several times quite softly all by itself in an atmosphere of complete and holy tranquillity. The repetiteur has it all to himself in that one place to create exactly the right atmosphere, and God punish him if he doesn't, as the beauty of the whole scene would be ruined.

(c) A melodeon, a small wind instrument with two octaves of keyboard notes, which is held in the left hand and sounded by depressing whatever note is required and blowing through a curved pipe, should be always on hand and available for the use of repetiteurs for the purpose of giving the pitch to all off-stage vocal music. This instrument can also be used where necessary particularly when a singer is very far from the orchestra and can't hear in *pp* passages. The repetiteur can usually be hidden behind part of the scenery for this purpose.

A new bell mechanism has been invented by Mr. Norman Feasy and had its first and comparatively successful trial at Covent Garden during the recent performances (1951) of Wagner's *Parsifal*. The chief advantage of Mr. Feasy's invention is that these "bells" (they are not bells but thin steel rods struck with a minimum of effort) can be played in the orchestral pit thus obviating the difficulty of off-stage risks. The sound of these steel rods is conveyed by microphone to loud speakers behind the scenes and can be played *pp* to *ff* at will.

Inherent in all off-stage effects—bells, cannon effects (*Madame Butterfly*), noises of people falling (*La Bohème* and *Figaro*), heated argument (*Manon*), etc.—is the element of exact timing. These effects *must* be controlled by repetiteurs and not by stage staff. The reason I lay down this definite ruling is that to my mind only a practising musician (in this case the repetiteur trained in an opera house) will feel the urgency of the *time element* in music at a given moment. In most of these off-stage effects *there is only one place*—maybe a split second—where the effect is truly realistic. If the effect takes place at exactly the right moment the dramatic realism will have its maximum intensity.

Other duties that the repetiteur will consider as part of his manifold activities are, playing the organ, celeste, signalling the exact moment for the raising and closing of the curtain to the stage manager. Many "curtains" are ruined by lack of exact timing. I could instance numerous examples of difficult "curtains" where a moment's hesitation will make the composer's intention null and void and make the artists on the stage both angry and uncomfortable. A repetiteur will therefore learn the speed of the opera house's curtain and consult the conductor with the stage manager and producer present as to the correct kind (slow or fast) and timing of all curtains. Proper rehearsals of the "curtains" should always be undertaken before the final general rehearsal.

Finally I would advise the would-be conductor to look upon his period of work as a repetiteur as a golden opportunity of learning all that is possible and, above all, of studying the conductor at work. In regard to this last point the repetiteur will be well advised to find out beforehand from the conductor of the opera concerned the correct tempi and nuances of a part and to follow out the conductor's ideas whether he agrees with them or not. Very often a tempo will seem wrong or slightly too fast or too slow to the repetiteur but he must always remember that the conductor in front, if he is a sincere artist, has worked out the question of tempi and has taken into consideration all sorts of factors which the repetiteur *has not yet experienced*. It is very easy to criticise the man in front but he must remember that the conductor's problems are many and varied. This view is not meant as a condoning of incompetency and should not *be understood as such*.

CHAPTER XV

THE PROPER ORGANISATION AND PERFORMANCE OF OFF-STAGE MUSIC AND EFFECTS

LET ME begin by stating that in many opera houses off-stage musical effects are performed in a perfunctory and haphazard manner, so much so that although more often than not the effects are musically in the right place the real intention of the composer, the creation of mood and atmosphere, is completely lacking.

I would take as an example of this the bells at the commencement of Act III in *La Tosca*. In this scene Puccini wanted each bell to sound as if coming from the churches in Rome at various distances from the fortress. Some of the bells are near and some are far away, some at the half distance. To do this correctly in order to create the real effect intended, each bell should be placed, in as far as is possible, at different distances, and thus in different parts of the stage, the orchestra (mainly the string section) meanwhile playing as quietly as needed. If this were carried out with care and the players properly rehearsed, there is no reason why Puccini's intention should not come to complete fruition.

But such is the perfunctory way in which this magical effect is carried out in some opera houses that for the sake of convenience all the bells are heaped together just behind the nearest bit of scenery facing the audience. In consequence not even by the longest stretch of imagination can the sensitive listener be persuaded that Puccini meant anything else than that a sort of humdrum bell concerto was meant to be performed. By the exercise of a little imagination and physical effort this scene could be an inspiring one.

In the same scene a boy singer is employed to sing a shepherd's song and sheep bells are heard as well. The boy and bells are in the same perfunctory manner situated behind the most convenient bit of scenery (which is by the way supposed to represent the immense stone tower of the fortress) so that all these effects if not done correctly make a mockery of the scenery. Even a child could see through the absurdity of such hoodwinking. The question which should be answered quite clearly is whether the opera house intends to present faithfully or not the composer's intentions and wishes.

Another effect in the same opera, in Act I, is that of the cannon of the fortress which is heard inside the church of Saint Andrea della Valle about two miles away. More often than not this cannon (a bass drum) is given a tremendous "swipe", again just behind the most convenient bit of scenery. The sound has little relation to the real circumstances. The church is built of massive blocks of stone and the character "Angelotti" taking refuge therein certainly *must* hear the cannon, but a sincere study of the *kind* of sound required and experimenting with various sizes of bass drums is urgently needed.

Some off-stage choruses require careful placing for the same reason. A far-away and distant chorus can seldom sound so when the chorus is too near the audience *even if they sing pp*. The audience is rarely deceived by such convenient practices. In my opinion no temporary solution can take the place of an honest one in creating atmosphere.

The obvious solution of this aspect of off-stage musical effects is the appointment of a musician who will make his whole-time work the study of such effects, rehearsing of same, and being on the stage to see his wishes carried out at every performance and listening when possible to the effect in the auditorium.

Apart from the repetiteurs who coach the singers, every large opera house should have about four or even six musicians who do all or most of the practical musical prompting and off-stage musical effects at all the evening performances. These "extra" musicians are used in all big and important opera houses on the Continent. They relieve the repetiteurs of such work and thus allow them to devote all their time to coaching singers.

In regard to prompting there is a mistaken idea prevalent in this country that prompting is infra dig. Such is the attitude only of those who fail to recognise the enormous difficulties to contend with on the large opera stage. At times it is almost humanly impossible for the conductor, at the great distance he is from singers at the back of the stage, whose view is often obscured by those in front, to control such large bodies of people to perfection. The level of the stage makes it an impossibility for every one to get a clear view in big crowd scenes and it is absolutely necessary for musicians to be posted at various points both sides of the stage in order to keep the chorus in time with the conductor. This kind of prompting or stage conducting has the added value of allowing much more natural freedom of movement on the stage. Even if the backs of the artists are turned to the conductor for production reasons, ensemble need never suffer as a result. One instance of this is the very difficult "swan" chorus in *Lohengrin*. The swan appears in the distance at the back of the stage and the male chorus *must* turn their backs on the conductor if the whole scene isn't to look completely absurd. But this method of off-stage conducting must be thoroughly organised and completely in line with the principal conductor. All the stage conductors must use "peepholes" in the scenery as a matter of course so that there should never be the slightest difference between themselves and the main conductor as to tempo and ensemble. In all these matters it is the standard of performance which counts. Perhaps the day isn't too distant when all off-stage choruses will be controlled by the main conductor with the aid of television equipment. If such a day does arrive electrical equipment will have to be more perfect than it is at the present moment. Fundamentally I have more confidence in human agencies in all these matters.

CHAPTER XVI

CHORUS MASTER AND CHORUS

MUCH OF the foregoing will apply to the chorus master's duties in an opera house. The chorus master is one of the most important appointments in opera and it is absolutely necessary that the right man should be found. He should be an enthusiastic opera lover. But much more than that, he should be a good pianist, have an impeccable ear, and if he has absolute pitch, all the better. There are many places in off-stage chorus work which are unaccompanied or almost so because of the distance from the orchestra. During the course of such performances if the pitch begins to flatten the chorus master should be able without instrumental aid to sing with the chorus and give the correct pitch to them. Loud-speakers or other such aids have a habit of breaking down, and without absolute pitch a chorus master can get into trouble. If a chorus master hasn't absolute pitch (and it doesn't follow every good chorus master has) he must use some instrument as a standby. The usual and best instrument for this purpose is a Mustel organ, or an instrument called a melodeon, which can be carried about with the greatest of ease. A chorus master should never be shy or afraid to use such an aid, as the final result is the thing that counts. Wagner himself directed that several instruments should play, behind the scenes, the opening of the Pilgrims' chorus from *Tannhäuser* as a surefire help until the chorus began to move on to the stage. At the other side of the stage either the same or another group of instrumentalists would be waiting to help the chorus when they sang the final few bars off-stage. This is one of the most difficult items that a chorus has to cope with, because during the walk *across* the stage, pitch can easily suffer. There is only one safeguard that must be taken relative to using instrumental aids for pitch. *This is that an unaccompanied chorus* must *sound* unaccompanied to the audience. The use of aids, whether horns or clarinets, *must* be inaudible in the auditorium.

Once off-stage chorus work is accompanied by the conductor in front, a beat must be passed to the chorus master and the tempo taken in this way. Too many chorus masters seem to think of their off-stage chorus work as being entirely under their own command and that, therefore, the conductor in front himself must endeavour to follow. This is an entirely erroneous assumption. Even the unaccompanied passages must conform to the conductor's idea as he is the one who has studied the work as a whole. It is artistically wrong for two conceptions to be going on at the same moment and this must be avoided at all costs. So it is imperative that the chorus master checks up with the conductor, after each act if necessary, as to nuance, tempo and ensemble. In this way the chorus master can eradicate misconceptions which may creep in during future performances.

The duties of a chorus master are both simple and complex at the same time. One could sum his work up in a sentence; namely, the perfection of chorus ensemble (attack, etc.), nuance and tempi with absolute musical accuracy.

He must set aside time for keeping the repertoire up to the highest standard even when he is teaching the chorus a new opera. He should, *before* teaching the chorus an unfamiliar work which is to be included in the repertoire, take the precaution of discussing the tempi and any other points with the conductor concerned, in this way ensuring that the chorus learn their parts correctly at the beginning, thus saving time and worry later.

The chorus master must be a disciplinarian, kindly but firm, understanding and approachable. He should be loyal, musically, to the conductors. He should be eager to protect the chorus from any injustice and see to their welfare on all occasions. He should on the other hand never allow any slacking either on the stage or in the rehearsal room, at all times suppressing the time-wasters and "talkers". He should assist the stage manager to ensure silence after each exit and before an entrance; to reprimand lazy choristers who don't "make up" correctly or who wear their clothes in a slovenly manner. He should do this by trying to instil a sense of pride in the heart of each chorister towards the important part that they play in the whole outcome of everyone's effort to create a perfect performance. He should instil loyalty and enthusiasm if it doesn't exist and in this he should be helped by the conductors. He should insist on the correct dynamics and nuances at each performance.

The chorus master should be present at all important discussions on the routine of the opera house.

As to the method of teaching the chorus, this can be left to him if the results are good. In this country we are in the happy position because of the great choral tradition which exists of being able to choose from many. And once having found the man with a high standard of choral and musical achievement, the only thing that remains is the question of his personality and ability to deal with the varied types in a chorus.

The size of a chorus often depends upon the ability to persuade the administrator to allot sufficient money for this purpose but, this consideration apart, I feel that a chorus should be at least one hundred and twenty strong if it is expected to cope with all chorus work. To me it is most inartistic that the chorus should be expected to represent two rival bodies in different scenes when anyone in the audience can tell they are the same lot of people who discard one costume for another. To quote a recent example in the production of Arthur Bliss' *Olympians* at Covent Garden, when Diana's entourage becomes later the followers of Bacchus *even without a change of costume*. How much more thrilling would it be when both sets of women in two big scenes eventually fill the stage for the final scene. Such scenes as the *Aïda* triumphal scene, and the last scene of *The Mastersingers*, are compelling and irresistible in the extreme with large numbers of choristers. Then there is a place in several operas for "children". All operatic chorus masters should deliberately choose several very short singers or even young girls for the important boys' chorus in *Carmen* and the children in *La Bohème*, only to quote these two operas.[1] The accepted custom of quite a number of opera houses in which outside bodies are used as "extra" chorus is only a half-hearted solution of the big crowd scenes contained in some of the bigger productions. Much better is the system in use by the Bavarian State Theatres

---

[1] I would go further and suggest that no big opera house should be without at east twenty-four good boys' voices.

in which pensioned-off choristers are expected to do service in crowd scenes. For especial effects where beauty of tone and quality of musical performance is necessary (*Parsifal* celestial choir, *Aïda* slaves, etc.) unless choristers can be spared there is no other solution than that of a trusted and musical body of singers from outside. But there are always small difficulties to encounter with outside bodies and the question to decide is which is the most satisfactory from the opera-house point of view.

In preparing a new work or a work not yet in the repertoire I would expect the chorus master to have his chorus ready before the ensemble rehearsals commence. He should pay meticulous attention to the composer's markings so that the conductor can add certain modifications as he thinks fit, such modifications to be rehearsed before the beginning of the final rehearsals.

The best choristers are those who have been trained to be *beat conscious*. At least I would go so far as to say that however excellent is the musically trained chorister, if he or she fails to understand or appreciate a conductor's beat all the musicianly training in the world will be well-nigh useless.

I would enjoin the chorus master to pay particular attention to the aspect of his work, training the choristers to recognise both this *pace* and the *length* of the conductor's beat.

Other points will be dealt with in the chapter on final rehearsals.

CHAPTER XVII

ORCHESTRA: LEADER: LIBRARIAN

THERE is very little to say on these points except that the choosing of an orchestra is a laborious and tedious business involving the auditioning of hundreds of unknown players, to seeking out the experienced players who will accept an operatic orchestral contract. It's just hard work, plus experience in orchestral technique, and a shrewd judgment. Many players (notably women) excel in auditions, and our conductor must be fully aware of this fact before passing final judgment on the poorer showing at auditions of other players.

The type of contract should undoubtedly consist of a weekly number of hours, with safeguards such as the length of each rehearsal (except the final ones) not to exceed three hours.

LEADER

The choice of leader is a vexed question. A leader is expected to be everything in a musical sense rolled into one. He must be a first-class soloist; a player with a great orchestral sense; a man of authority and personality respected by all. He should insist on a routine of tuning; should set certain rules of behaviour at rehearsals and performances. He should stamp out all unnecessary noise and "preluding" at rehearsals and performances, and should insist on complete silence when the auditorium lights are lowerd preparatory to the commencement of each act. Such discipline has a chastening effect on garrulous members of the audience as well, and gives just that tranquillity before music "breaks the silence".

One of the explicit duties of the leader is to arrange with the conductor *before* orchestral rehearsals the bowing of all string parts. This should be done in time for the librarian to mark all copies for such rehearsals.

Orchestral Intonation. Various methods have been suggested to settle the variations among orchestral players as to correct intonation. Several conductors have suggested ways and means as to how this can be achieved. Many players will remember Sir Henry Wood's insistence that tuning must be done in the bandroom and his method was to go among the players before each performance with his huge tuning fork and hear each instrumentalist sound his 'A'. Many are the stories told of this. The trouble always was the difference in temperature between the old Queen's Hall bandroom and the hall itself. Players would often have to make further adjustments when they sat in their places on the platform.

Scherchen advises at least twenty minutes "warming up" in the bandroom and further suggests that each family of instruments should get together and test their intonation by playing various chords or passages in the works to be played. This is indeed as near perfect a method as possible of getting correct intonation. But I wonder if it has ever worked? or ever *could* work? There is so much going on just before a concert in the bandroom. Players don't all arrive at the same time. Unless the bandroom was divided into three or four enclosed sections it would be very difficult to employ this method for the simple reason that the noise would be cacophonic and no one would get a correct idea of intonation.

Too frequently the oboe player and the clarinets are at variance. Flutes and clarinets need great care. If one could insist on a proper drill, each section tuning in turn and then together under the leader of each section, it might be possible to adopt Scherchen's suggestion. It would be a great advantage to do so. This method of tuning is adopted by the orchestra of La Scala, the brass particularly spending at least an hour together before the performance. Consequently intonation was perfect in every department of the orchestra.

Players must be given credit for wanting to be in tune with one another but often don't succeed in being so. The only practical suggestions I can offer are: firstly that there should be someone responsible for watching the temperature of a band-room and that such temperature should be as near as possible (by controlling the heating) to that of the auditorium; secondly, that the leader should make it his business to insist on the players tuning to a tuning fork before going on to the platform.

Thirdly, that when the orchestral players have seated themselves and when the leader is settled, a further *quiet* tuning should take place. The leader and the first oboe player will arrange when this should take place. After this all tuning and certainly any "preluding" should absolutely cease. The band-room tuning fork should be a very large one about six inches in height mounted on a large box enclosed on all sides except one. A slight tap from a drum stick will give a long and loud note, the box acting as a resonating chamber. On the platform by the leader there should be a small fork of a similar kind, which could be tapped quietly after the first item is over. This second tuning can be carried out quite unobtrusively.

The tuning fork I have in mind and which I had first made to my own specification was made by Boosey & Hawkes (or perhaps it was by Hawkes & Sons, Denman Street) and proved of great value, and settled many an argument between players.

For the rest of this question I can only suggest that the young conductor should strive his utmost at all times to produce perfect intonation at rehearsals, and set some sort of system whereby this is carried out before performances. He can do no more than this and if his players are conscientious enough and the leader insistent enough the problem will be solved to the credit of all.

LIBRARIAN

In a big opera house the librarian will need at least two assistants. There is the orchestral side of the library, the vocal score section, including chorus parts, and the writing in of translations. The librarian must make all cuts correctly and in good time for the opening rehearsals. He must see that all vocal scores that are bought are the correct edition. He must find out from the conductor concerned the correct cuts and each copy loaned to the artists correctly marked with the translation clearly written in. Each copy must be signed for and collected after the last performance of the opera and all losses made good.

The librarian should be a good copyist, or at least one of his assistants should be. He must see that, when necessary, extra markings (nuances, etc.) should be inserted after each rehearsal. It is advisable that the librarian should attend all orchestral rehearsals so that changes found necessary should be marked in before the next rehearsal. It is also advisable that the librarian should not be a member of the orchestra, but should have had a good orchestral experience.

I think that some better method of handling orchestral parts should be devised than the present one of tying up a whole set of parts with string and thereby cutting into the edges of parts until after frequent use the parts become badly cut and torn.[1] A strong folding canvas case with ribbons for tying up could easily be made, thus adding years to the life of a set of parts. Another duty which is imperative is that of a close inspection of parts and scores every now and then to make good any torn leaves. The librarian should put in all bowings in the string parts decided upon by the conductor and the leaders of each string section.

[1] This bad practice exists in a number of theatre libraries throughout the country. How much better is the attitude towards orchestral parts in the German opera houses where each set of parts is contained in a canvas-bound box.

CHAPTER XVIII

ARTISTS

WE HAVE had it levelled at us in this country that we are not operatically minded and that we haven't the singers to build up a great operatic tradition. The trouble is that there are not too many people who frequent our opera houses who have enough confidence in the ability of our British singers to bring our great experiment to fruition. When one thinks of the British National Opera Company which at Covent Garden performed in its stride (1922) the whole of the *Ring* in English, uncut, conducted by Englishmen (Coates, Pitt, Buesst, Harrison, Goosens Jun.) and that also the repertoire included all the usual Wagner operas, all Verdi's big operas, all Puccini had then written and many British, Russian and French operas. When one thinks of this and the standard achieved by this company one is inclined to be both angry and full of a chuckling mirth at the innocence of our detractors. The B.N.O.C. just didn't *suddenly* become an opera company but was the result of fifteen years or so of continuous effort on the part of Sir Thomas Beecham and his father Sir Joseph Beecham. Singers were found and taught their art. Where there is a strong enough demand, so in some miraculous way the supply is created. The same thing could happen now and in fact *is* happening now at Covent Garden. We must make the opera-going public aware of our task. They must become identified with our ideals by taking a conscious part in encouraging our new singers. The so-called star system or guest system is, except in some cases, a bad principle when building up a native operatic tradition. We must remember that we in this country are only going through *now* what Paris, Vienna and the opera houses in Germany all went through at one period of their operatic history when Italian opera and Italian singers were predominant in every opera house worthy of the name. Opera in those days was only sung in Italian and each country in turn saw the necessity of putting a stop to such a ridiculous state of affairs. Gradually native singers were found who learnt to sing convincingly in their own language and opera composers no longer were compelled to write operas to Italian librettos. The result is that we now have a repertoire considerably enriched by composers who were not writing in a foreign language, and each with something different to contribute.

Singing in English has been decried by many people but who can say that the beautiful language of our poets really presents any difficulty? One of the faults has been bad translations, but that difficulty is not insurmountable. The whole point is that opera has now become part of the ordinary citizen's life and if we are to fill our opera houses we must present our repertoire in English. The first step has already been taken and indeed partly solved by the excellent work of both Sadler's Wells and the Carl Rosa opera companies. The position at Covent Garden is somewhat more involved. Opera is presented in English there but too often with foreign artists making valiant efforts to overcome difficulties in pronunciation. The foreign artists' attempts are very often half-hearted, but the English singer is *expected* at times to sing many operas in languages they don't thoroughly understand, which is equally absurd.

What we really need is a fund for training young artists who give successful auditions, instead of, as at the moment, not engaging them because we can't displace artists already under contract. Many young artists could be trained at this school and gradually worked into the repertoire, first of all in small parts under the eyes of the conductors, after which a round-table discussion should take place as to the next step. The "school" should consist of repetiteurs and producers who would be charged with the task of preparing these young artists for their rôles. What may happen if a young artist gives a successful audition is that he or she is hurriedly put into a part without due preparation—very often with no stage calls—and through sheer fright half the value of the voice is lost, after which the conductor becomes antagonistic or afraid to risk another such performance. Then the young artist is neglected and not used. We expect far too much of the inexperienced artist.

The "school" should be part of the opera house organisation and, be it noted, *not a school for singing*. The one object of the school would be to teach the young artist operatic parts, small at first, so as to fit him or her by gradual stages to become a useful member of the opera house.

(2) Having set out with the ideal of building up a National British Opera how must we go about it? I think we can ignore the people who cry out for opera in its native language. One has only to look at the situation on the Continent where, in France, all operas are performed in French, irrespective of their country of origin. The same applies to opera in Italy, Germany, Russia and other countries. That each of these countries has also a big repertoire of its own is most fortunate, and it is our misfortune that *at the moment* our own repertoire of operas by native composers is both small and, with few exceptions, not universally widely known or popular. This state of affairs is being gradually overcome and several operas by native composers are beginning to take their place in our repertoire. But side by side with this growth of English opera is the building-up through experience of our British operatic singers. The two objects should progress together, but I am inclined to think that the most determined efforts should be directed towards our singers. Our audiences must be brought into our scheme. They must be told that at Covent Garden the wasteful days of the "Grand Season" (except as a short tag-end to the yearly season) are over and in its place we intend to search the country and the Dominions for outstanding talent until in a few years we will have the finest body of singers in the world. In the meantime we may make a few mistakes, we may even have to employ some guest artists, but our final object will be unchanged. There are many artists in this country who *should* be singing opera but because of difficulties in negotiation are not doing so. In this way some of our best artists are lost to us. This difficulty must be overcome and every inducement offered to bring these artists into the fold.

Side by side with our problem in London there is the crying need for two or three subsidiary opera establishments in the big cities in the provinces and Scotland. But not until the problem of artists is solved in London would it be wise to expand elsewhere.

(3) Having covered, however imperfectly, the issues at stake in London, the only point to consider now is the practical side of the problem with particular reference to the body of artists and their work.

The repertoire of operas must be chosen to satisfy two ends: (a) the capacity of the artists to interpret the rôles given them, and (b) the appetite of a public already brought up on the operas that have thrilled audiences all over the world.

In other words you cannot open an opera house to the public unless you give the well-known works and with singers who can sing them. This may or may not clash with our ultimate ideal and the public being what it is we must steer the ship very carefully. On the other hand it's no use filling your season with operas for which an adequate cast is not available. I could think of several operas I would like to perform but unless I had the singers in the opera company who could do full justice to the rôles it would be useless to put the opera down for performance. The "guest" system only partially solves the difficulty because more often than not the guests are unavailable when they are most wanted, particularly for rehearsals.

(4) First of all an ensemble must be built up. Taking as a basis the usual operatic repertoire comprising the well-known works of Puccini, Verdi, Wagner, Mozart, Rossini, etc., and adding during the first five to ten years other works such as operas by Massenet, Charpentier (Louise), Borodine, Tchaikovski, etc., and new operas by British composers, we would need a body of singers comprising two experienced dramatic sopranos, two lyric sopranos, two mezzo-sopranos, two contraltos, four tenors (two dramatic, two lyric), three baritones, two bass baritones, three basses, as well as numerous artists for character parts and smaller parts. With these experienced singers should be the second ensemble of younger singers from the school who would understudy big rôles and play very small parts, gradually being given more responsibility as they became more experienced.

The staff of conductors should watch closely over the interests of the younger artists, encouraging and advising them in their problems and supervising the work of the school.

(5) The training of the artists must be strict in every way. The repetiteurs must insist on absolute musical accuracy, not

passing *a single mistake* at their rehearsals. The first and foremost need is to instil the greatest respect for accuracy with particular reference to ensemble. Each artist must learn his or her part so accurately that mistakes made by other artists should never deter them. The foolish habit of learning word cues and blindly following the other singer's mistakes is fatal. All parts should be learned away from other singers, and intervening rests or bars counted as an integral part of the rôle. When this has been done and the part memorised the next step should be to bring the singers together. In other words the individual artist should learn never to rely on anyone else on the stage. He or she should be able to cover up any mistake by being as "firm as a rock" musically. It is to the cultivation of this musical certainty that the maximum efforts of the repetiteur should be directed. Artists will bless them later on even although they may seem at the time to be harsh taskmasters. I contend that if a part *has* to be learnt it is just as easy to learn it correctly as incorrectly. So why not learn it correctly in the beginning? Unaccompanied bars of a singer's rôle where the notes form a definite musical shape should be learnt as the composer wrote them. The composer thinks in terms of musical shape continuously throughout a work and goes to the trouble of thinking out the best music pattern and shape for the words. He further goes to the endless trouble of laboriously writing notes with stems, with ties, with all sorts of differentiating signs according to their value. Whatever do you think he does this for if he doesn't mean it? One very good example of this kind of thing is the opening of *La Bohème* where there is quickfire repartee between Rudolph and Marcel entirely unaccompanied for many bars and where Puccini has written every phrase in a predetermined shape and furthermore has written "sempre a tempo", which is often ignored by the two artists concerned who entirely misread the wonderful idea Puccini has put down on paper for their benefit.

I feel sure that the two singers (Rudolf and Marcel) both, perhaps unconsciously, feel that for a short space they are relieved from the "tyranny" of a conductor's beat and quite erroneously also feel that by singing these passages ad lib they are getting more expression into them. A quite mistaken idea and most disloyal to Puccini. The bars in question form a bridge passage between two orchestral outbursts and are *not free in any sense of the word*, yet one is frequently exasperated by singers who ignore Puccini's wishes. The unfortunate point about this passage in question is that the conductor is powerless to intervene or influence the singers *during* the performance but must take them to task later when the damage has already been done. The wayward singers and the singers who either can't read music or have never given music serious thought *must* be treated with the sternest discipline for their own sakes. For this reason the opera school should prove of extreme value in teaching the young singer operatic (and therefore musical) discipline.

Discipline

There are two aspects of discipline most desired in the opera house. I have spoken of musical discipline but there is another kind of discipline which is just as necessary. The kind of discipline which determines the whole attitude of the artist towards his or her work and towards the opera house. When simple rules are made by the director and their being carried out insisted upon by the executive staff with the director's full support, all artists will develop a sense of responsibility which will stay with them wherever they go and in whatever conditions they may work. Some artists have this feeling of responsibility born in them, others need it thrust on them, and for the sake of good operatic work all artists must subscribe to it. There should be someone or several people from the administration who should be in attendance at all rehearsals to see that discipline is maintained and who should take artists to task when any one of the rules is broken. Any artist continuously breaking these rules should have fair warning, after which, should the artist continue to be at fault, disciplinary action must be taken.

I imagine that every opera house has unwritten rules which are insisted upon, but at the risk of seeming to be tiresome and boring, I will enumerate what I feel are the most important ones. The word artist includes anyone taking part in rehearsals and performances.

(1) Every artist is expected to be at the rehearsal at the time stated.

(2) Irrelevant conversation at rehearsals not allowed and to be immediately stopped and artists warned of the consequences.

(3) Every artist should sing full voice in ensemble rehearsals but especially with orchestra when the question of balance as between singer and orchestra has to be assessed.

(4) During stage rehearsals no artist not actually taking part at that moment should be allowed to be in or walk across the acting area of the stage.

(5) During stage rehearsals the strictest silence to be observed by the artists.

(6) At final rehearsals all artists must act and sing as at a performance.

(7) At final rehearsals and performances all artists must use full make-up and wear their costumes in their entirety.

(8) Absolutely no noise or conversation either on the stage or behind the scenes during performances unless such is required by the producer. (This is particularly necessary during orchestral preludes or just before "curtain up".)

(9) All artists must be present at curtain calls as arranged by the producer or stage manager.

(10) All artists at performances are expected to sing and act to their full capacity and to carry out their work as directed in rehearsals by the conductor and producer.

(11) All artists are expected to request an interview with the conductor or producer after a performance if he or she has committed mistakes. (Such interview should be regarded as an opportunity both for an apology and a "checking up" as a safeguard in future performances of the same opera. It will also prove the artist's full sincerity and eradicate any impression to the contrary that may arise in the conductor's mind.)

(12) All artists are expected to know their rôles from memory before ensemble rehearsals commence.

(13) All artists must acknowledge the authority of the stage manager during performance when any order given by him must be obeyed instantly.

The Rights of the Artist

Artists should have the right of insisting on more rehearsal if he or she thinks rehearsals have been insufficient.

An artist should have the right of refusing to sing a rôle if he or she can prove that such rôle would be damaging to his or her voice.

An artist should be able to refuse overworking his or her voice.

No artist should be called for long rehearsals on the day when he or she is singing a big rôle that evening and it is advisable that:

No artist except in emergency should be called to rehearse a *different* opera from the one he or she is performing in at night *especially if the evening rôle is a major or exacting one.*

These are just a few points which as a general rule are observed in most opera houses.

SINGING TEACHERS

Although I do not advise interference in any way with an artist's choice of singing teacher, in practice, if an artist's voice is showing signs of wear and tear or the bad result appears to be wrong teaching, interference becomes a necessity. If this arises the administration has the right to cancel a contract if the artist refuses to leave his or her teacher.

On the other hand the director should have the right to insist that an artist goes to a singing teacher if he or she is not working with one already.

Good singing teachers are rare but there are a few and these should be known by the opera administration and artists sent to them if necessary.

CHAPTER XIX

THE PRODUCER

Every conductor of opera should also be a producer of opera. I mean this absolutely and literally, and for the following reasons.

An opera conductor if he is any good at all and has studied his operas deeply and with understanding, can see into the composer's mind with unfailing judgment. He can see the composer's reason for many musical passages which are an enigma to the non-musician. The composer (especially of modern operas) visualises in his own mind the movements of his singers on the stage. *He is his own producer while the work is taking shape.* If the conductor has honestly studied an opera to the full he must visualise the composer's own production because in almost every bar he can find musical illustration, both of the thought going through the minds of the characters, and of their movements. To take a very small incident, that of Mimi's fainting (Act I, *La Bohème*), when Puccini gives to two solo violins (pizzicato) four notes which one immediately associates with Rudolf's action of flicking a few drops of water on Mimi's face in order to revive her. I remember once taking over *La Bohème* from another conductor and finding this very necessary bit of business omitted. Naturally I reinstated it. Now why was this omitted? Both musically and by Puccini's own instructions set down in the vocal and full scores he has asked for it. Surely the answer is, either the producer concerned hadn't read the score (which seems so fantastic that it can't be true!) or he didn't understand what the art of opera means. Many other omissions one could quote, one of them quite fantastic in its idiocy: in the death scene of *Boris Godounov*, when Boris points out to the Boyers his son and says, "There is your Czar" the producer insisted (although the composer had written it down in the vocal score to the contrary) on the Boyers being off-stage so that Boris was left talking into thin air. Such producers may be tolerated in the straight theatre but in opera the music and the composer's instructions are a continual reminder that he (the composer) had the original ideas and some producers can't bear the idea of sinking their own individualities in that of a man, perhaps long since dead. Personally I insist that the composer is right every time even if, as has happened on several occasions, his meaning is obscure. I have always found that in time the composer's idea reveals itself clearly. I remember another instance in the second scene of Wagner's *Tannhäuser* when the producer passed the scenic designer's setting of the wayside shrine (at which Tannhäuser prays after his deliverance from the toils of Venus, and towards which the pilgrims genuflect on their way to Rome) right at the back of the stage, making it impossible for the artists either to hear the quiet playing of the orchestra or even see the conductor. The Pilgrims also had to turn their backs to the conductor! This had the effect of shattering the musical ensemble, difficult enough at this point, and, as well, most successfully endangering intonation. Wagner has clearly written his instructions in both the vocal and orchestral scores but on this occasion the scenic designer and the producer turned the whole scene round the wrong way. Wagner was an operatic conductor and knew all the possible difficulties to be encountered. As a result of this incident just quoted a rule was made that the conductor concerned should see models of the sets and discuss their practicability from the composer's point of view. This was carried out and it was most instructive to learn how scenic designers can go astray. Previous to this rule operatic sets were made after approval by the producer alone and very often it was found out too late that the poor artists had to sing under the most uncomfortable conditions.

I hope I am not giving the impression that I am against the scenic designer and the producer showing originality. On the contrary I am all for the utmost originality being squeezed out of a well-known work. What I entirely disapprove of is that the producer should alter specific instructions laid down by the composer or should insist that artists move *aimlessly* about while singing. There are producers who cannot leave music alone to tell its own tale. We all know that if the opera was a drama instead we would expect the actors to be more natural-istic, but (how silly it sounds!) opera is not drama alone—it is far more difficult. As I have said elsewhere, there are five arts which go towards making an opera but by far the most important of these is music.

When I laid down the dictum that "every operatic conductor should also be a producer" I meant what I said. As to whether a conductor, except in exceptional circumstances, would have time to both produce and conduct is another matter. But if he is not the producer also he must at least stop producers from ruining the musical score. Again to quote an instance, I remember seeing the ending of Strauss's *Salome* completely ruined and rendered meaningless by a producer's "brilliant" and "original" idea (on paper or in his mind) turning out to be absolutely funny. Another instance of ignoring the composer's written instructions. Strauss has laid it down that Herod orders his soldiers (who have been standing watching Salome's ghastly kissing and gloating over Jochanaan's severed head) to kill Salome, and in a flash and as a result of this horror the deed is done and Salome is crushed and stabbed to death. This is the only fitting end to the horror of the scene and is the one redeeming feature of it. It makes sense psychologically and in some way it satisfies our idea of punishment fitting the crime. But on this occasion the producer dispensed with these silent witnesses (the soldiers) and out of nowhere appeared two "supers" with enormous spiky shields bigger than themselves (nicknamed the "Nuremberg Maiden") which, despite every effort of themselves and of the Salome never once suceeded in giving the impression of crushing her to death. How much better Strauss's (and Oscar Wilde's) direction! The look of growing horror on the faces of the soldiers and their eagerness to carry out Herod's order lends truth to the horrifying scene.

It is an interesting fact that when human beings are asked to do something which they feel instinctively is wrong or unnatural they never succeed in making it convincing.

The more one studies the question of production in opera, the more one is surprised to find that there are so many opportunities given by composers to producers. The composer as a rule writes his instructions sparingly and simply. One of the most ingenuous yet vital descriptions—almost classical in its understatement, is that of the second Polish scene of *Boris*

Godounov. The composer has written "The garden of Sandomir castle. Moonlight and a fountain". In one production I saw of *Boris* there was neither fountain, garden, nor moonlight. The castle which should have been seen in the distance was transplanted almost on to the footlights. Such are the foibles of scenic designers! Moussorgsky's music, which is wonderfully descriptive of moonlight in some miraculous way only great composers have, was married to a scene which was entirely antagonistic to it. Anyone with knowledge of Moussorgsky's music could never have passed that scenery, and that kind of fault in a producer is of a fundamental kind and stamps him as one who is not "cut out" for opera. Taking Moussorgsky's instructions (above) all the producer has to do is to see that the scenic designer makes an appropriate set. He can show only half the castle either on the right or left of stage or even only one wall or a tower; he can let his imagination run riot with the garden; he can put the fountain almost anywhere so long as there is sufficient room for the singers to move. The mistakes he *could* make are many and manifold. The fountain could completely dwarf the set; if it was a heavily built structure, shifting it into place after the previous scene would make the interval too long and it would also occupy too much room on the side of the stage when not in use.

The mobility of scenery even on stages with modern mechanical devices is most important. Long intervals can turn a good opera into a failure with an audience which must get home at a reasonable hour. If there is more than one scene in an act the sets must be so devised that the shortest time is taken in shifting from one to another. When a short scene is followed by another scene which may be more grandiose and bigger, the first scene must dispense with anything in the shape of built-up sets so that the transition to the next scene takes place with a minimum of strain and in as short a time as possible. I once saw a production of a well-known opera when the interval times added together were longer than the opera itself.

If big built-up sets are to be used, then they should be used for an opera in three acts and three scenes only. If the opera house has both the sunken and rolling stage it is possible to do much more.

LIGHTING

This question of scenery is a most important one to the conductor for if the sets are not of the right kind the effect which the composer intended to create will be blunted or completely lost. Nothing can be more disconcerting than when all one's efforts go for nothing. Even lighting is important. There is a moment in the last act of *Manon* where a star suddenly shines through the clouds and de Grieux speaks about it. At the moment this star appears Massenet has written a few notes on divided solo violins in the upper register with a tinkling chord played by the harp. (Once again we are amazed at the simplicity and wonderfully descriptive perfection of the great operatic composer.) If the star appears a second too late or the light itself is of a dull yellow colour the magic of this effect is lost. The music is the key to the effect—it is bright and scintillating—but to a lighting expert it is only an electric bulb and once having done his job in providing one, any kind of criticism of the colour seems to him to be both finicky and unnecessary. But as a conductor of opera I cannot stress too strongly the tremendous importance of these effects and their relation to the musical score.

Chapter XX

SCENIC EFFECTS

Now I come to a point to which I have given many years of thought. So many operas which have become part of the permanent repertoire have in them some kind of what I call extra-scenic effects. I could list many such, but just to mention a few, we have the distant appearance of the swan in *Lohengrin* and its gradual growing into life-size until its entrance with Lohengrin onto the acting area of the stage; the magical transformation of the swan into the dove in Act III; the "visions" in the Venusberg scene of *Tannhäuser*; the ghostly ship in *The Flying Dutchman* and the "apotheosis" at the end of that opera; the toad in *Rhinegold* (usually left to the imagination and darkness); the flames in *Valkyrie*; the ravens in *Götterdämmerung* and the overflowing of the Rhine at the end of that opera; the waves and tide filling the cave at the end of Ethel Smythe's opera *The Wreckers*; the Paris firework scene in *Louise*; the rising moon in Act II of *The Mastersingers*; the fireflies in *Madame Butterfly* and *Hansel and Gretel*; the flight of the witch in *Hansel and Gretel*; the "Fire and Water" scene in *Magic Flute*, etc. etc.

As a general rule attempts have been made by German scenic designers and producers in the thorough manner of German technicians to *solve* all these effects in Wagner's operas and to a great extent (at least in Germany) very successfully. Quite often, outside Germany, these effects (in Wagner's operas) are laughed at as being rather a little bit childish and are therefore done badly or, as in the case of *Lohengrin*, left out completely. Generally the technical staff of an opera house is far too busy with ordinary everyday lighting to give enough thought to these "extra-scenic effects" and gradually there grows up complete indifference to them and they are left unsolved or done in a perfunctory manner, consequently losing most of their value. The main point is lost sight of—that the composer has written descriptive music for these effects, and the poor conductor has to "plough" through music which has, as a result of these half-hearted solutions, become meaningless.

What is the solution of this state of affairs? There is only one. Commencing with the dictum that the composer is always right and all effects (whether scenic or musical) should be done in as realistic a manner as possible, a body of technicians should be formed from the technical staff with any outside help that is necessary and a member of the musical staff, whose main work would be the study and solution of these problems. The appearance in the distance of Lohengrin and the swan, its gradual growing to life-size is not such a difficult problem, yet I remember two productions in this country in which the effect was completely ignored. Even the final appearance of the swan itself has been badly done, with the boat being unevenly pulled and as a result, moving in a series of epileptic jerks. I can imagine how foolish and silly the "Wolf's Glen" scene in *Der Freischütz* would look if done badly. One must take these things seriously. For good or ill the composer's music has been written around these childlike stories and legends, and once the music is accepted everything else *must* go with it.

As a rule these effects are left to chance and there is sometimes no time to make them realistic before the first performance. Here is where the value of my suggestion would come in. Long before the rehearsals of the opera had got to the final stages this body of technicians should have been working at the "extra-scenic effects" and have perfected them in time for the assembling of the stage sets. It is all possible given time, expert planning and determination.

CHAPTER XXI

PRODUCER AND CONDUCTOR

LITTLE remains to be said in regard to this subject except perhaps a few words dealing with the question of combined rehearsals with producer and conductor. The invariable rule is that the conductor should insist on the artists being note-perfect before the producer has anything to do with them. I shall have more to say about this later, in the final chapter dealing with rehearsing an opera. But there are, however, a few important points to be remarked upon about these joint rehearsals.

When the artists have completed their rehearsals with the conductor, they should be left for a while to the producer so that he can explain his ideas and put them through their stage business. Sometimes, and whenever possible, the producer can take solo artists through their acting work even while the conductor is still rehearsing other members of the cast *so long as the artists already know their music*. This last injunction is imperative and should never be departed from.

Then after the producer has taken the whole cast and chorus through their stage work the conductor should rejoin the rehearsals and *supervise the producer's work*. Here the conductor (as he is *not* the producer of the opera) must confine himself to making suggestions as to the better positioning of the artists where necessary so that they can give their full attention to the music. Sometimes a conductor will have to *insist* that the producer alters the positioning of the artists and until this is done the rehearsal can't go on. There are other times when although the position of the artists are dramatically perfect and even musically speaking are quite natural and good they may have to be altered for reasons of balance and difficulty of musical ensemble. Often artists have to be brought nearer the footlights because the original position, although dramatically perfect, did not allow their voices to be sufficiently heard above the general ensemble. Mostly on these occasions common sense wins the day but if the producer is inclined to be stubborn the conductor *must* for the sake of musical ensemble have his way.

The conductor should start with the assumption:

(1) That the first and foremost element of importance in an operatic performance is that the voices must be heard.

(2) That movement *must* coincide with the appropriate music.

(3) That exits and entrances should be at exactly the right moment musically.

(4) That rarely should the artists be expected to turn their backs to the conductor when an important or difficult entry is about to be sung.

(5) That all fussy and over-complicated "business" during musical ensemble should be eliminated.

(6) That the movements and steps of the chorus during musical ensemble should be so arranged that at the important musical entries they should have a clear view of the conductor and that such movements or steps at the moment of singing should stop or be greatly simplified.

(7) That when the artists or chorus have a running entry onto the stage this should as far as possible *anticipate* the musical entry.

(8) That all choristers and artists in big ensembles *who have the same musical part should be together in their respective groups.* (This can often be a bone of contention between conductor and producer but here again the conductor must insist on a re-grouping for the sake of perfection of musical ensemble.)

In regard to (7), very often, for the sake of dramatic verisimilitude, the chorus and artists have to march or walk to a rhythm or even run onto the stage. Care has to be taken that a clear idea of tempo is instilled into them so that their movements as far as possible should conform to the correct tempo. In illustration of this I remember taking over another opera when the producer in a big crowd scene had given the chorus quick and violent movements during a tranquil chorus folk tune. The movements were so instilled into the chorus that the correct tempo was impossible. The conductor on these occasions *cannot* sacrifice tempo which is inherent in the very tune itself. So the expedient of arranging for some choristers to

move and the others to sing was resorted to. A case in point
where this is imperative is the "Quarrel" chorus at the end of
Act II of *The Mastersingers*. The fight proceeds merrily during
the most difficult ensemble ever written in which nearly a
hundred people take part and it is literally impossible to
demand musical perfection while there is such a swirling mass of
people moving on the stage. What usually happens is that the
apprentices, and the ballet dressed as such, do all the fighting
in the foreground, while the chorus proper and the "Masters"
stand still and do the singing. Another difficult place occurs
in the last scene of the same opera when David is dancing a
vigorous waltz with one of the maidens from Fürth and while
doing so is expected to sing some most difficult entries. This
is one of the places where the artist must be very quick and
certain, for *dance he must*.

In many places in opera there are no instructions as to stage
business written down by the composer. Generally speaking
the composer and original producer have conferred during the
first rehearsals of a new opera and the stage business has therefore become a tradition which is handed on down the years
but has become altered by successive producers and artists until
the point of the original "business" has often lost its meaning.
When this happens the new producer has a perfect right to
infuse his own ideas into the production so long as he does not
go contrary to the composer's *written* instructions. For instance
there is no valid reason why the producer shouldn't instruct the
designers to put the window in the Act I of *La Bohème* on the
left instead of the right. But even this seemingly innocuous
alteration creates unexpected difficulties, in that in opera,
tradition has played a tremendous part in production all over
the world and when an artist comes into a changed production
(in the case of emergency) the whole of his or her performance
is handicapped by the strangeness of unfamiliar sets.

With a play the matter is quite different. The production in
this case is for a run—be it a week or a year of the same play.
In opera the whole basis is repertory—a different opera every
night. This therefore narrows down the extent of the producer's
originality. Apart from this I do not believe originality, either
in sets or production, is such a simple matter as that of turning
the sets around. Originality in scene designing is more a matter

of architecture, perspective and colour, always keeping in mind the period of the opera and the country in which the plot takes place. For instance in *Boris Godounov* the scene of Boris's death is in the council chamber. Originality here is strictly limited. The prints I have seen of this chamber are quite stark enough without the imposition of any Freudian nightmare. Marina's boudoir (*Boris Godounov*) is nothing more than that, although colour and architecture can play a great part in its originality but it must be an enclosed set that can make way in a few seconds for the following scene. In a recent production of *Boris* the producer passed the scene designer's highest flights of idiocy. The "boudoir" on this occasion looked more like the steppes of Central Asia in the depths of winter. The fantastic and lunatic height of incompetency being reached by the ladies' costumes being designed for the warmth of an indoor scene! Marina on this occasion was sitting on a swing, the ropes of which had no visible means of support but as far as one could tell were hitched on to stars way up in the heavens.

Originality in costume has to be very carefully considered. Costumes, especially of the fifteenth, sixteenth, seventeenth and eighteenth centuries, are sufficiently colourful in themselves to be copied as faithfully as possible and thus give pleasure. I have known scene designs (and costumes) to be entrusted to surrealist artists who have made mincemeat of the period of the opera. In other words originality in this way can, as I have pointed out elsewhere, ruin an opera.

So the whole problem boils down to the choice of producer. If he is a man fully in sympathy with opera he will scrutinise the scenic designer's work, insisting on alterations where the designer has contravened the composer's instructions or tradition and put nothing better in its place. After this has been done and the finished models have been inspected by the conductor and the technical staff *then and only then* should the sets be built and the costumes made.

There is, of course a wonderful opportunity in legendary and mythical operas for scenic designers and producers. Costume for this style of opera has fallen into accepted styles, usually flowing garments for women, and skins and such like for men. Scenery for these works is as a rule of a rugged nature and the imagination of the scenic designer can run wild.

One last word in regard to the lighting of sets. As I have pointed out before, lighting is part and parcel of the music and in parenthesis may I beg producers to make up their minds as to the *time of day* in their lighting of scenes. Unless the scene is meant to have no relation to real life, some sort of timing and movement of light consistent with the actual position of the Sun in its orbit should be attempted. I have seen in some productions the dawn come up on both sides of the stage: likewise the Moon has shone from every direction. The whole purpose of normal lighting as distinct from phantasy is to imitate nature's own colour scheme and movement.

I remember the first time I saw the (then) new sets for the *Ring* at the Prinz Regenten theatre in Munich in the year 1922. What struck me at the time was not so much the beauty of the sets and the solution of each technical problem of lighting and scene changes, but the wonderful reality of the dawn effects. I felt that the lighting experts had *really seen* and *timed* a dawn—that it was the result of real knowledge. It wasn't just a make-believe of the usual change from blue and rosy pinks to sun-up. There were many combinations of colours such as one *does* see in a dawn. Wagner has given two wonderful opportunities to the lighting experts in the *Ring*, and they, the experts, had taken them with both hands. Other extra-scenic effects were just as well done, notably the ghostly ship in *The Flying Dutchman*. Here the appearance of a ship ploughing through the sea with the waves parting at the bow was simply and most realistically portrayed by having a huge balloon, the size of the acting area of the stage, partially filled with air, which gave the ship rolling over the top of the balloon pushing the air before it, the impression of great speed and billowing waves. The technical staff had solved this problem, always a difficult one, in a most expert way.

The waves and rising tide in the cave in Act III of *The Wreckers*, by Ethel Smythe, was partially solved in two ways. On the ground cloths and low stage sets, painted to look like waves and pulled higher and higher from the "flies", a cinematograph photo of waves was projected and rice thrown into the air to give reality to the idea of the sea breaking against rocks. Combined with this the noise of the sea and the cries of sea gulls was superimposed by a loudspeaker from an H.M.V. record actually taken in Cornwall.

This was done at Sadler's Wells during the year 1938 and considering the resources of that theatre was quite a remarkable effort. The chief point I wish to make is that a real attempt, quite successful in its way, was made to solve a difficult problem. In those days although the theatre didn't boast a special "extra-scenic-effect" staff the result was the same for the simple reason that all ideas were tried out.

Chapter XXII

POSITION OF OFF-STAGE EFFECTS

THERE are certain stage (musical) effects that must be mobile. For instance, if the bells are always kept in the one place there will be occasions when the sound obviously comes from the wrong side of the stage. To obviate this, sets of tubular bells can be put in any position so that the sound appears to come from just the locality required. Another instance of the positioning of off-stage musical effects is the cuckoo in *Hansel and Gretel*. I have played this instrument on the passage right above the scenery so that the sound appeared to come from above. The trumpet call in *Fidelio* announcing the arrival of the Governor to Leonora, Florestan, Rocco and Pizzaro, who are in the deepest dungeon of the prison, should always be played as if it came from above, and the only way to do this is for the trumpet player to play it in the same passage above the scenery.

So, musical off-stage effects must not only be played at the right moment but also, as far as possible, in the right position.

There is another question in regard to off-stage music which needs airing. This is the extreme difficulty encountered by repetiteurs in finding room enough or peace enough to do their work properly. Some operatic stages or stage designers (bless 'em) have never made provision for off-stage effects. Single bells, gongs, cannons, etc., are easy enough, but when you have whole orchestras behind stage, sometimes with twenty-five to thirty players, space is rarely allowed for players to play in comfort. I will instance several operas where there are groups of players behind stage, in explanation of a suggestion I would make in regard to a possible solution these difficulties.

Tannhäuser, horns in Act I, and the two orchestras under stage at the end of Act III.

Tristan, trumpets, etc., at the end of Act I, and horns in Act II.

Lohengrin, trumpets, trombones, etc., in Act II.

Siegfried, horn in Act II.

Götterdämmerung, "cow horns" in Act II.

Parsifal, trombones and bells in Act I.

Boris Godounov, complete sets of deep bells in *great numbers*. (This is essential if the sound of all the church bells of Moscow ringing out for the Coronation of the Czar are to sound in any way realistic.)

La Tosca, bells of the churches of Rome in Act III.

La Traviata, orchestra in Act I.

Rosenkavalier, orchestra in Act III.

The difficulty with all the above instances of off-stage music effects is that in most opera houses they are played behind the scenery on the stage itself and on a stage that is overcrowded with scenery and built-up sets, thus making it sometimes a nightmare for both the players and the off-stage conductors. This difficulty was partially solved in the Staatsoper in Hamburg by having a big chamber built *behind* the conductor and *underneath* the first five or six rows of the stalls where almost every musical effect could be coped with in comfort. This chamber was so built that the sound impinged on to the stage and the audience was deceived into thinking it came from it. This chamber solved at the same time the difficulty of transference of beats, because everyone could *see* the conductor and played directly from his beat. Even some of the off stage choruses could be accommodated in this chamber.

When I mentioned that this chamber was only a partial solution of the problem I meant that in quite a lot of cases many off-stage musical effects would still have to be performed on the stage because of the desire for musical realism. How can this be done so as to allow for the comfort and tranquillity of the players and musical staff? There is only one solution, and that is the construction of two or three musicians' galleries built into or projecting from the side and back walls of the stage itself. These galleries should be placed high enough to leave room for scene shifters and stage staff working below. They should be roomy enough to allow for the biggest off-stage combination of instruments or chorus. Every possible type of off-stage musical work should be envisaged when they are planned.

It is quite possible that a projecting gallery would be a nuisance; if so, the idea of inset galleries built of the correct

material and so shaped that the sound travelled on to the stage
would be the best idea of all. In such galleries the musicians
with their music stands, chairs, etc., could do their work without worrying about the crazy turmoil that goes on during
scene shifting. This idea is worthy of serious consideration.
How much better to have the *Parsifal* trombones played in
one of the side galleries or even in the back wall gallery
behind the stage, whereas at the present time they are
played in a passage in discomfort.

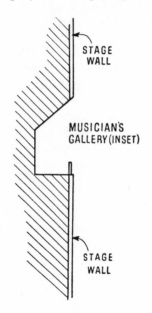

STAGE WALL

MUSICIAN'S GALLERY (INSET)

STAGE WALL

It is my contention that the stage
of an opera house should be planned
always *with the repertoire in mind.*
There are certain operas that require
much more space for their performance than others. There are
some operas that have special off-
stage effects for which especial provision must be made. Most stages
are built with only the scenery
and lighting in mind. Big musical
off-stage effects have usually to be
performed wherever room can be
made for them. To take one specific
example, let us consider the performance of *Parsifal.* Off-stage effects
are: the trombones (already mentioned) in Act I; the deep bells;
the celestial choir; the voice of
Titural, not to mention the pan-
oramic change of scenery in Act I (not by any means an
off-stage effect; it takes place in full view of the audience).
These *Parsifal* off-stage effects require proper arrangements
made for them; a gallery for the trombones; a proper carillon
of deep bells slung from a batten; and another gallery for the
celestial choir, the sound of which should come as if from the
dome of the building. As it is the trombones are played in a
passageway, the bells higgledy-piggledy on the floor of the
stage or some other improvised position always in the way of
the scene shifter, and the celestial choir lumped together in any
odd space where possible (in Covent Garden this was usually

in the paint room where the air was full of the smell of size used for mixing paints).

The carillon of bells is the necessity of every opera-house stage. For *Boris Godounov* every variety of deep bell should be used including the *Parsifal* and *Tosca* bells. Either a gallery for this purpose or bells slung from an immense batten at the back of the stage is required. (Even deep gongs mix very well.) If the complete set of *Boris*, *Parsifal* and *Tosca* bells are slung from a batten these can be lowered to stage level when required and pulled up out of the way after use. It all should be so simple: much simpler than the laborious business of the bells being carried by the property staff backwards and forwards for every performance. The only difficulty in this is the weight of the *Parsifal* bells. These are enormous and very heavy, and some other means may have to be found to house them on the stage, but the point is that this problem must be grappled and dealt with to the satisfaction of all.

In the Berlin State Opera and the Paris Grand Opera a complete carillon of bells for every purpose so far envisaged is in use. The sound of these bells is produced electronically and is as near to the exact sound as human ingenuity has been able so far to produce.

Chapter XXIII

ORCHESTRAL PIT

SOME orchestral pits are just like a huge gaping mouth some-what distorted. Some of them have had chunks taken out of the walls so that more players can be accommodated. Some are architectural monstrosities and shapeless holes. An orchestral pit should be a well-shaped chamber where the orchestral player can feel some sort of pride when he enters it. There should be ample room even for the largest orchestra to play in comfort, for the simple reason that when players are comfort-ably seated and have ample room to play in, the best work will come from them. The horribly uncomfortable oblong shaped pits are a misery to both players and conductor. The conductor in such a shaped pit feels he is at a tennis match at Wimbledon twisting his head from side to side following the play.

There is only one good shape for an orchestral pit, the half-moon shape, giving the greatest distance between the con-ductor and stage, and bending inwards towards the ends where the space will be less. In a pit so shaped there will be ample room in the middle of the pit for the octet of wood-wind at the back of the violas, where they are directly under the eye of the conductor.

PLAN OF ORCHESTRAL PIT

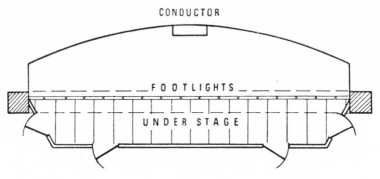

142

The elevation of the pit is another important matter both from
the points of view of line of sight (of the players) and balance of
tone.

In my proposed orchestral pit the brass instruments would
be under the stage (below and behind the footlights) in much
the same position as at the Bayreuth Festspielhaus and the
Prinz Regenten Theatre in Munich, although the complete
covering of the orchestra in those two theatres is a matter of
opinion. Personally I think it would be an easy matter to have
a cowl on the outer rail of the orchestral pit which could be
pulled up for the *Ring* and lowered for other operas.

The elevation of the pit should be so arranged that the
stringed instruments will be one step higher than the wind
with the brass a step lower than the wood-wind.

ELEVATION PLAN OF ORCHESTRAL PIT

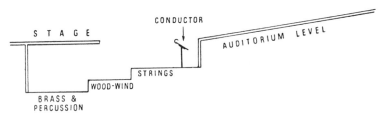

The "placing" of the orchestra is a matter of conflicting
opinion, but given the half-moon shape as advocated above and
taking into consideration the question of proximity of each
family of instruments to one another, combined with their
lay-out from the conductor's point of view, the best placing
of all is the usual symphonic one used on most concert platforms.
(See plan on page 144.)

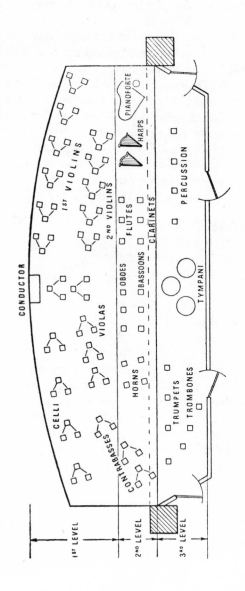

Chapter XXIV

MUSICAL ORGANISATION OF THE OPERA HOUSE

HAVING considered the production of opera from every angle as it affects the musical side I feel it is necessary before discussing the business of rehearsing an opera (which is the main point of everything that has been written up till now) that we should have a clear idea of the duties of the musical staff relative to the routine of an opera house.

On the one hand there is the administration dealing with the manifold items connected with an opera house: the building; contracts; choosing of personnel in every department and seeing that contracts are fulfilled; and lastly, but most important of all, assessing the value of every person working in the opera house. Under this heading comes the enormous responsibility on the artistic as well as the financial side.

Directly under this are the two main departments, production and musical. The plan at the beginning of this part of my book dealing with opera will give a clear idea as to how and into what categories these two main departments divide.

The musical department of an opera house consists of:

(1) The musical director.
(2) The conductors.
(3) The chorus master and chorus.
(4) The repetiteurs.
(5) The artists.
(6) The orchestra; leader; librarian.

The duties of (3), (4), (5) and (6) have already been discussed. All that remains is to discuss the duties of (1) and (2).

Let us take the musical director first. His main duty is to insist that the routine of the musical work of the opera house is properly carried out.

He should plan all rehearsals in consultation with his musical staff so that each conductor and each opera irrespective of the conductor should have thorough rehearsal. He should not favour any particular work or conductor, for to him the reputation of the opera house depends on thorough rehearsal and every endeavour should be made that every performance should be as perfect as possible.

In building up a new operatic tradition the essential thing is that every member of the musical side should work together as a team. The system in vogue, for instance, in Germany of the "Herr General Musik Direktor" being the one conductor to take over all important operas having thorough rehearsal for them, with the other conductors taking what is left with inadequate rehearsals, is completely out of place in our present state of operatic progress. The musical directors of our opera houses have something far more important to do. To them belongs the colossal task of building up an operatic tradition from "scratch", as it were, for the simple reason that, apart from the valiant efforts of the touring Carl Rosa Opera Company, the only two opera companies which functioned *as* opera organisations were the B.N.O.C. which ceased operations in 1928 and the Sadler's Wells opera house which broke up in 1940 but has since been reorganised and is doing most valuable work. Sadler's Wells, as a matter of fact and history, from 1931 till 1940 made enormous strides and I for one believe that had it not been for the war (1939–45) would have had to move to a larger theatre and would have become the mainspring of our national opera.

Since 1946 the operatic situation has completely changed with the formation of the permanent opera at the Royal Opera House where the resources for great performances of opera in English are well-nigh limitless and the future of opera on a permanent basis in this country is well on the way to becoming assured.

So, rightly or wrongly, I believe that the paramount duty of the music director is to organise to perfection the musical routine. If this becomes his main function there cannot be much time left for him to conduct. His main duty for several years will be to attend rehearsals, to supervise the work of all members of the musical staff; to apportion rehearsals equally;

to hear new singers; to intervene where necessary for the better ordering of everyone's work; to see that the musical staff have every assistance in the carrying out of their work; to advise the administration on all musical matters. If he has still time left to conduct some performances it would be all to the good. He would not lose any prestige by waiting until the organisation of routine *was on a firm basis*.

THE CONDUCTORS

In a big opera house there should be three conductors, each chosen for his ability to drive through all obstacles and achieve good performances. But their work could become a series of frustrations if the musical director was biased or didn't give them the utmost help and encouragement. On the other hand the musical director must be firm and untiring in his efforts to see that the conductors give of their best. There are many instances during final rehearsals when it is of the utmost help if the musical director is somewhere in the background listening to the effect from the auditorium and advising the conductor as to better positioning of the artists or the balance as between orchestra and singers. Also the advisability of asking for more tone from off-stage choruses if necessary. In fact the musical director can give invaluable help in many ways. I firmly believe that the conductor concerned should have this backing, especially during final rehearsals when nerves are at the breaking point and it just needs a spark to start a fiery outburst *which seldom does any good* just at that moment. The conductor, surrounded by and having his ears filled with the sounds coming from a big orchestra, especially when the auditorium is empty, can miss some very important aspects of balance. Here the musical director can help to make or mar a performance, but if this authority is not forthcoming the conductor must himself become the musical director for the time being, and should be invested with the complete authority necessary.

One final point and a very important one. Each conductor should have the same amount of authority in his own right. No one conductor should be allowed to "pull strings" at the expense of the others or for his own aggrandisement. I re-

member seeing in an opera house which shall be nameless a
notice put up on the notice-board that "artists must not leave
Mr. So and So's rehearsals at any time without *his* express
permission" instead of as it should have been: "No artist
can leave any rehearsal without the *conductor's* permission."
The first kind of wording immediately segregated the afore-
said conductor into the one who had the *only* authority and
the others who were not allowed any. A notice of this kind is
bad for general discipline throughout the theatre. It teaches
the whole staff to be on the qui vive for the one person and to
slack for the others, which after all is completely detrimental
to the general standard.

INTERCHANGE OF OPERAS

To keep the conductors, singers and orchestra fresh, a certain
amount of changing over of operas from half-way through a
season is essential so long as it can be done without unnecessary
rehearsal. Such interchanging is good from other points of
view. It gives each conductor a chance to enlarge his repertoire
and prevents him from getting stale. In cases where it is
obvious that a conductor has made a particular success of a
work he is tremendously fond of, it is very difficult to do this,
but if he is being offered another opera he has never conducted before, he should be well satisfied. It also means that
in emergency the other conductors are fully qualified to take
over an opera. It would also mean that each conductor would
become interested in his colleagues' work, whereas very often
the opposite is the case.

This interchange I feel should only apply to the operas that
are very well known and which are the pillars of the repertoire.
Perhaps the rule should be that any opera which has been in
the repertoire for three years continuously should be ready for
an interchange of conductors. This interchange of operas
brings with it the vexed question of individual interpretation
which is the only point that may create difficulty. But as artists
are interchanged (and their interpretations are usually quite
different from one another's) so there seems to me to be no
valid reason why conductors shouldn't interchange. If the
changeover is done in the middle of the season no major

alterations should be allowed. If, on the other hand, a different conductor takes over the opera at the beginning of the season, more liberty should be allowed to him because of the long interval since the last performance and the possibility of adequate rehearsals.

Chapter XXV

ON REHEARSING AN OPERA NEW TO THE REPERTOIRE

Now WE come to the all-important discussion towards which everything so far written has been directed. Not until every aspect in the routine work of an opera house has been touched upon would it be possible to discuss and lay bare the many intricacies in the preparation of an opera' for performance. Not without understanding how the whole machine works, how every cog fits into the wheel, would it be possible to write down with clarity the many ramifications of this vast undertaking. Having somewhat cleared the ground and prepared the soil we now have to commence planting the right kind of seed and must watch over its growth. To make our discussion worth while we will choose an opera full of difficulties, with a big cast of singers, several changes of scene, problems of lighting, extra-scenic and musical off-stage effects, and a difficult full score.

The choice of opera hardly matters except in one particular, namely, that it must give complete scope for discussion and should embrace all difficulties encountered in an opera house. The field is wide open for our choice but I am going to choose a well known opera for the simple reason that a full score will be available for the young conductor and he will be able to follow any references with comparative ease.

We can't do better than to choose *Tannhäuser* by Richard Wagner. In this opera you have a big cast with difficult ensembles; with off-stage choruses; with ballet; with "visions"; with a quick change from the Venusberg to the wayside shrine scene; with hunting horns off-stage; with massive chorus work on-stage; with stage trumpets off- and on-stage and with the two small orchestras under the stage in Act III; with Venus appearing and singing at the back of the stage while Wolfram struggles with the soul of Tannhäuser in the foreground; and the gradual filling of the stage towards the end with the Pilgrims returning from Rome.

Each opera has its own peculiarities and not all problems are the same but I think that *Tannhäuser* is as interesting a choice as any.

PRELIMINARY DECISIONS

The committee of the opera house, which should include musical director, conductors, chorus master, producer, scenic designer and stage director (who meet at least once every week and decide on choice of opera, singers, producer, conductor, etc.) will have got down to their work at least four months before the date of performance. All details having been settled, it remains for the conductor, producer and stage director to choose the earliest date for inspecting the scenic designer's models. When this has been done and the conductor has at the same time worked out his scheme of rehearsals, a plan should be drawn up on the following lines (see page 152) and issued to all departments. This plan may have to be altered drastically, because one must remember that other operas are being rehearsed at the same time, and it is only for the guidance of conductor, producer and stage director in the preliminary stages, and will be absorbed later into the main scheme of rehearsals by the music director.

After this provisional plan has been submitted to the musical director a more complete plan including all the rehearsals going on during the same period of three to four months showing the complete working of the opera house should be drawn up on a much larger sheet but worked on the same principle. (See page 153.)

This plan can be worked either monthly in part detail or three monthly with only the main items for rehearsal. The plan itself is only a guide, but a very good one, and from it the weekly call sheet should be made out in complete detail. The chief value of this plan that one can see at a glance is the *time limit* imposed on the executive staff in getting the familiar, the new (new in the sense that they come into the repertoire for the first time) and unfamiliar works on to the stage.

PLAN OF OPERA REHEARSALS I

TANNHAÜSER

WEEK	SOLO	CHORUS	ENSEMBLE	PRODUCER	SCENERY LIGHTING	ORCH.	FULL MUSIC	FINAL REHEARSAL	PERFORMANCE
1	TANN	TANN			PAINTING ETC				
2	TANN	TANN							
3	TANN	TANN	TANN.						
4			TANN						
5			TANN.				TANN.		
6			TANN.	TANN. (SOLO)	↓	TANN. (SECTIONAL)	TANN.		
7				TANN. (DUETS Etc)	ASSEMBLING SETS	TANN	TANN		
8				TANN. (FULL)	LIGHTING	TANN			
9				TANN (FULL)		TANN			
10					↓	TANN 2	TANN 2		
11					TANN.	TANN 2	TANN. 2		
12					TANN	TANN. 1	TANN 1	TANN	
13								TANN	
14									TANN

Note. All other operas being rehearsed at the same time are eliminated in this plan for the sake of clarity.

PLAN OF OPERA REHEARSALS II

showing full scheme of rehearsals in fourteen weeks

WEEK	SOLO	CHORUS	ENSEMBLE	PRODUCER	SCENERY LIGHTING	ORCH	FULL MUSIC	FINAL REHEARSAL	PERFORMANCE
1	TANN.	TANN.	CARMEN BUTTERFLY	→	TANN.	CARMEN BUTTERFLY	→	→	
2	TANN.	TANN.	TRAVIATA ←	→		REPERTOIRE		CARMEN BUTTERFLY	
3	TANN.	TANN.	TANN.		CARMEN BUTTERFLY			TRAVIATA	
4	ROSENKAV ← →		TANN.						
5	ROSENKAV ← → BOHEME	BOHEME	TANN. ROSENKAV				TANN		CARMEN BUTTERFLY TRAVIATA
6	ROSENKAV ← → BOHEME	BOHEME	TANN. ROSENKAV	TANN. ROSENKAV	ROSENKAV	ROSENKAV	TANN ROSENKAV		
7			BOHEME	TANN BOHEME ← → BOHEME			ROSENKAV	ROSENKAV	ROSENKAV
8	WOZZECK			TANN		BOHEME ← → BOHEME			
9	WOZZECK			TANN					
10	WOZZECK					TANN ← →		BOHEME	BOHEME
11	WOZZECK					TANN ← →			
12	WOZZECK		WOZZECK			TANN ← →			
13			WOZZECK			TANN ←		→	
14			WOZZECK						TANNHAUSER

Note. New works in repertoire underlined, unfamiliar new works twice underlined.

Certain works can never be regarded as easy to put on.
La Bohème, Falstaff, Boris Godounov, Fidelio need a proper
routine of rehearsal every time they are done and cannot be
skimped. Other works are much easier once the initial difficulties have been overcome.

Chapter XXVI

DUTIES OF THE EXECUTIVE COMMITTEE

Before laying down the routine to be followed in rehearsals, a word needs to be said about the executive committee and its function. This committee should consist of the musical director, the conductors, the producer, the chorus master and the stage director. They should meet once a week and always on the same day and hour. A proper agenda should be followed and minutes kept of each meeting. Subjects for discussion would be: the daily reports from the repetiteurs; the nightly reports on each performance sent in by conductor, producer and stage manager; the progress or otherwise of the artists; criticisms of performances; results of auditions; the weekly call sheet; and any other business connected with the day-to-day routine of the opera house.

Three months before the end of the season the same committee with the addition of the administrator should sit three times a week in order to fashion the following season's work; to discuss the whole range of the present season; to decide on the new works and the dropping of others; to cast all operas up to the end of the first three months of the following season; to decide on conductors, scenic designers and producers for the new works (a list of which should be drawn up from suggestions received from outside bodies, conductors and producers). Each conductor and producer should take time to think about these new suggestions and should be prepared to vote for or against each one. The choice of new works must be influenced by what is best for the ensemble of artists in its present state of experience with the view towards their progress as a whole and with an eye on the public as well. Mistakes can be made, but if the executive staff is actuated by the desire to build up a perfect ensemble and is imbued with the strongest manifestation of team spirit, all will be well.

Chapter XXVII

THE REHEARSALS IN PROGRESS

Now LET us discuss the rehearsals of *Tannhäuser* in some detail. Once the routine has been fixed it only remains to follow the course and outcome of it.

Firstly the casting is of the greatest importance. One thing you can be sure of: without the right singers the work had better be postponed.

For Tannhäuser, a tenor of the Helden-tenor type is essential.

For Wolfram, a bass-baritone with a melting type of voice and a calm personality is needed.

For the Landgrave, a bass voice and a man of commanding presence.

For Bitterolf, a baritone able to act in a forthright but somewhat truculent manner.

For Walter Von der Vogelweide you would need a young tenor voice and a young ingenuous type of actor.

Schreiber (a tenor) and Reinmar (a bass) can be chosen from the remaining members of the ensemble.

For Venus, especially as we propose that the Paris revision be performed, a dramatic soprano of power is required. She is also expected to be a woman of exceptional beauty of form.

For Elizabeth, another soprano, dramatic but of a fuller quality of voice, able to sing the "Prayer" in the last act with soft beauty of tone yet able to penetrate through the big ensemble in Act II with ease.

The Young Shepherd (a soprano) should be chosen from the "school" and she should be a singer with a very good sense of pitch for she sings unaccompanied for long periods. She must also be entirely "safe" in her music.

Having decided on your cast, your plan of rehearsals should be drawn up as outlined in Plan I above. This should be submitted to the musical director who will probably adjust it in relation to the other works which will be rehearsed during the same period.

As there are so many parts (six in all) of the male ensemble the whole of the six repetiteurs will each take one of them individually in their solo rehearsals. But before this is done there should be a meeting of the repetiteurs and chorus master with the conductor who will impart the tempi and any other ideas he may have as to style in the performance and interpretation of the work.

To the chorus master for instance he will explain that although he is free to look after his Sirens' chorus and small orchestra behind scenes (page 59, full score, Fürstner Edition), he must work to a beat for the first nine bars and at the eighteenth bar, when the harp of the stage orchestra and the orchestra in front come together, he must again conform to the conductor's beat. But *there must not be any deviation of tempo* in the bars between. On page 64 he can again take over responsibility for the second Sirens' chorus. For the third Sirens' chorus on page 88 it is not strictly necessary to take a beat from the front. He should be warned of the difficulty he will encounter after the Young Shepherd's song on page 121 in that the cor anglais is usually played near the shepherd on the other side of the stage and that both he and the repetiteur responsible for the cor anglais player should be quite certain they understand that the rallentando of the cor anglais eventually becomes the slower tempo of the Pilgrims' chorus. He should be enjoined to create the effect of the Pilgrims coming from the Wartburg and that the *p* of the first entry is quite a different thing from the *p* when they are on the stage. During the long and chromatic section (third line, page 121) the tendency of the chorus is to go flat, so that at this point especially it would be wise to use the horns as a safeguard. Usually the Pilgrims begin to make their entry on to the stage during the last two phrases when they are singing in unison—often it has been found a safeguard to send on the first group and keep back the second group to finish the last phrase. During the next few bars when the Shepherd sings, followed by Tannhäuser, there is almost time enough for the Pilgrims to travel across the stage and get to the other side for the remaining off-stage music. Here again the chorus master should create the effect of the Pilgrims going on their journey and as a result the voices should seem to disappear in the distance. Once again it should be pointed out that Wagner's *p* here is only relative. That is the nuance the *audience hears*, but the amount of tone given at the beginning of this final off-stage will be considerably more so as to allow for such fading away. On page 187, Act II, care should be taken that the four notes of the ∽ should be sung on the second crochet every time; that the first part of this chorus is really only *mf* and that the entry of the male section on page 190 should be both robust and *f*. In fact all the few written nuances of Wagner (*p* on page 192, *ff* on page 194) should be strictly observed, and the last four bars on page 199 should be most brilliant in their intensity of tone—in fact *only here* should the *utmost* tone be given. All the short interjections from the chorus in Act II should be precise and incisive. On page 234 when the women rush off they must sing first and *then* rush off. Wagner has actually directed this to be done. The next entry of men on page 235 must be safe and exact.

The ensemble beginning on page 248 is full of interesting and most potent nuances to which the chorus master will be advised to attend. It is interesting to note that Wagner cut out all other voices but Tannhäuser's from page 253 onwards until page 257, when the Minstrels re-enter. A comparison with the first version will show that contrary to popular belief Wagner wasn't averse to making cuts.

The singing of the older Pilgrims who enter later with the body of Elizabeth (on page 354, Act III) is accompanied by four trombones. One wonders if Wagner put these trombones in purely as a help to the chorus or not, for at that moment there is no particular musical reason why the trombones in the orchestra shouldn't play instead. Be this as it may, after-thought or not, the trombones are a great help. (Care must be taken to give great solidity to the change from $\frac{4}{4}$ to $\frac{6}{4}$ on page 364, Act III.)

To the repetiteurs it should be pointed out that each member of the ensemble must know his part thoroughly. Reinmar and Bitterolf in particular have many similar "leads" and must not be brought together in ensemble until they are as firm as a rock musically themselves.

The repetiteur entrusted with the coaching of the artist who is to sing Wolfram should *consciously* instil into the singer's mind the equable, calm, generous tranquillity of the character. He should also teach him the movements he must make when, in Acts II and III, he is supposed to be playing the harp. After a while the orchestral harpist should rehearse the "Hall of Song" scene (Act II) with the artists, but this will come later during ensemble rehearsals.

Bitterolf's character is much more choleric and rough. He is the one who in the "Hall of Song" is not afraid to challenge Tannhäuser's criticism of Wolfram's idea of love. He it is who kindles the fire which sets Tannhäuser extolling the lusts of Venus. His *style* of singing and characterisation must leave an indelible impression on the audience. Walter (who was, by the way, the master of Walter von Stolzing, the hero of *The Mastersingers*) is a young man, gentle and artistic. His one song in Act II was subsequently cut out by Wagner in his Paris revision but I used to include it because I felt that although the singing contest may to some people seem protracted, yet without Walter's song it becomes nothing else than a quarrel between Bitterolf, Wolfram (to a lesser degree), and Tannhäuser. (This song is printed in the original edition.)

The character of the Landgrave should be a commanding personality, with a powerful voice, dignity of character, yet stern when required.

The two women, Venus and Elizabeth, are as different as night from day. Venus should be the embodiment of pleasurable lust and enjoyment, of a destroying, but fascinating, yet fatal beauty; the princess of sirens and destroyer of men's souls through both their bodies and minds. Is it any wonder that the more mature Wagner should be dissatisfied with his earlier music in depicting this paragon of lusciousness? All the honeyed sweetness a woman singer can manage to put into her voice will never be enough to portray the power of Venus over men. Yet something approaching it must be done, for characterisation in opera is one of its most potent factors.

For Elizabeth the repetiteur's task is somewhat easier. Her character is the womanly antithesis of Venus. She is calm, generous-hearted, forgiving and pure. She loves Tannhäuser with all the purity of her simple nature but will never understand the turmoil in his heart.

Tannhäuser is a lost soul from the very beginning of the opera, but somewhere inside his brain he knows that love must be unselfish to be real. He is torn between the lusts of the flesh and Elizabeth's purity, but like someone who has tasted the depths of degradation and sensuous pleasure he knows he is doomed. His journey to Rome to plead forgiveness from the Pope for his sins is the one redeeming feature in his character and only by his death can he be free.

As a singer Tannhäuser must be of the robust type. This is a very heavy part vocally and the "path to Rome" scene in Act III will call forth all his vocal and histrionic powers. This is one of the greatest solo scenes in the whole range of opera and woe betide a Tannhäuser who fails to rise to the opportunities presented to him by the composer.

The above few remarks are only a very inadequate résumé of some of the main characteristics of some of the characters and what is expected of them. Wagner himself has written a detailed analysis on the performance of this opera and no conductor should think of commencing rehearsals before he has read it. (See Wagner's prose works.)

As the weeks go on and the repetiteurs' reports on the progress of the artists begin to take a turn for the better, the conductor should then take a hand, and about the third or fourth week ensemble rehearsals should commence. First of all the Minstrels, Walter and Schreiber, Reinmar and Bitterolf, Wolfram and Landgrave, should be brought together in pairs for a few rehearsals, until they have acquired a certainty that is unshakable. Then a whole week should be spent on nothing else but the ensembles of Acts I and II. After this the chorus (having previously been taken through their work by the conductor) should join the Minstrels, and with the addition of Elizabeth and Tannhäuser, the two selfsame ensembles must be perfected. While this has been going on, the "duet" scenes between Tannhäuser and Venus, Tannhäuser and Elizabeth, and Tannhäuser and Wolfram should be thoroughly rehearsed. Finally the "trio" in Act III with Venus, Tannhäuser and Wolfram will need careful attention.

All is now ready for the final music rehearsals, and it is advisable to take each act in turn and not pass to the next act until every musical point has been settled and the singers have a firm grasp of every detail of nuance and tempo. This should be continued until in one or two rehearsals of three hours with an interval of a quarter of an hour it would be possible to go straight through the opera. Then and then only should the producer take a hand.

While the producer is taking the artists through their stage business the conductor should attend the ballet rehearsals. I fear I have a lot to say about this, especially in regard to *Tannhäuser*. The *Tannhäuser* ballet is not, in the strict sense of the word, a ballet at all. Yet how often does one see the usual ballet steps foisted onto this most wild of Bacchanalia? No! the *Tannhäuser* Bacchanale is the wildest, fiercest, Dante-like furioso ever conceived by an operatic composer. The whole theme should be a reflection of Tannhäuser's experience—tantalising, futile embraces, voluptuous movements and movements of complete abandon yet with never a hint of satisfaction. The women dancers should be dressed in as flimsy a one-piece covering as possible. The men's make-up should be as devilishly unsatisfied in expression as paint can make it. Satyrs and Fauns, Nymphs and Sirens mingle in fantastic movements, first of all in a frenzy of mad pleasure but later, as the music becomes quieter and more sensuous, in appropriate and lingering embraces of the most passionate nature. All this is written down by Wagner and makes sense of the music, surely the most expressive of its kind ever written. (The ballet arranged by Frederick Ashton to Liszt's "Dante" Sonata is the type of choreography required.) The chief point that the conductor *must* make quite certain of is that this Bacchanale should be done by the best dancers the opera house can provide. He will set the tempo with the choreographer and watch over it from the beginning.

The next thing to which the conductor will turn his attention (or relegate to a member of the musical staff) will be the rehearsal of the "visions" in Act I, but by this time orchestral rehearsals will be due to commence.

ORCHESTRAL REHEARSALS

Tannhäuser is in places technically very difficult, but with long stretches of slow-moving music which present no difficulty beyond correct balance and tone.

L

It is advisable to rehearse the strings separately as they have by far the most difficult passage work to contend with. Sectional rehearsals are essential in the early stages and a great saving of time, but they should take place concurrently; that is, while the conductor is taking the string players an assistant should take the wind players. Special attention will have to be given to the harpist and solo rehearsals with the singers will be necessary.

After the sectional rehearsals the orchestra will be brought together and the main orchestral rehearsals will commence. At a later stage the two off-stage small orchestras should join the main orchestra under the principal conductor, and the repetiteurs responsible for these two orchestras should sit each with his own orchestra and practise "passing the beat" to it. *Tannhäuser* will probably need six full orchestral rehearsals of three hours each before the singers can join. Altogether, counting the four sectional rehearsals (two for each section), this works out as thirty hours all told. Added to this will be three three-hour rehearsals, one for each act with the singers, and another two long rehearsals during the final complete rehearsals. The young conductor will get a good idea of the immense labour involved in the musical side of an operatic production by adding up the number of hours necessary in orchestral rehearsals alone.

Final Rehearsals

Before the orchestra comes to its final rehearsals the conductor will have rejoined the artists and producer for the combined music and stage rehearsals.

If all has gone well and the producer has made good progress, these rehearsals will be far advanced and all the conductor has to do is to co-ordinate more closely the music with the stage business. He may have to insist on slight alterations; he may have to repeat over and over again some of the really complicated places until they are right. He will certainly have to make quite certain of the Pilgrims in Act I and see that the question of intonation is not left to chance.

All these rehearsals will be done with a piano in the orchestral pit with the conductor conducting from his usual place. In this way the artists will get used to looking at the conductor at the difficult moments. It is essential that the rehearsal pianist at these final rehearsals should be thoroughly conversant with the conductor's methods and idiosyncrasies of tempo and he should feel the strange difference between the sound of the piano and that of the orchestra and should make allowances for it. He should never be allowed to play an important musical lead, on which the singers will depend so much, in a slovenly or unrhythmic manner as this will tend to make them unsure and unsafe at the performance.

The conductor at these rehearsals, after having been a stern taskmaster in the beginning, should begin to build up the confidence of the singers both in themselves and himself so that they approach the final rehearsals in a spirit of enthusiasm and certainty. I have seen some conductors bully their singers to such an extent that all the "fight" went out of them, and the very thing he himself desired most, a brilliant performance, became, on the first night, a most terrifying experience for all.

CHAPTER XXVIII

FINAL GENERAL REHEARSALS

EVERYTHING the conductor has worked for: the untiring efforts of the artists: the long hours standing about, with the nerves of everyone taut and maybe on edge, until, finally, the time has arrived for the supreme effort of everyone. This is the moment when the conductor must leave all thoughts of failure behind him; he must encourage his singers; he must even *not see* certain things which are too late to be altered. If he has worked faithfully and fearlessly all through the preparation of this opera he can do no more. If he has made a mistake in casting which has become apparent too late there is nothing much he can do, unless it is so bad that something must be done quickly. If he has been sincere in his approach to his work (and we all can make mistakes, more often than not through our sincerity), and has helped his artists rather than bullied them, he will not have many qualms of conscience.

Then what more can be said as to the conduct of these final rehearsals? Everything with off-stage scenic and musical effects will go wrong at first and must be rehearsed again and again until everyone knows exactly where the pitfalls are and how to circumvent them. The conductor should never say to himself "*that* will be all right on the night". "*That*" can go just as wrong during performance as at rehearsal. The chorus master must not allow himself to think that as the Pilgrims' chorus has kept its intonation right up to the final rehearsal that *that* fact alone will save him from criticism if they lose their pitch at the performance. Safeguards must be arranged for, but if not used, the chorus master can thank his lucky stars, for the time being, if no accidents have happened. No chances should be missed when instrumental aids to pitch are available.

The places for transference of beats in Act I are: the Sirens' chorus in Act I, Scene I; the second Pilgrims' chorus with violas and cellos in the orchestra on pages 122 and 123 (full score); the first and second entries of the off-stage horns on page 124 until the Allegro $\frac{2}{4}$ when the conductor in front can safely leave things to the repetiteur in charge. For all the off-stage horn fanfares from page 148 onwards a beat *must* be transferred.

In Act II, although it is not strictly necessary for transference of the beat at the first trumpet entry behind scenes, the ones that follow at the beginning of Scene IV, page 182 (full score), must all be taken from the conductor in front, after which the trumpet players should stand in a single rank at the back in full view of the audience. The long "Bach" trumpets should be used for these fanfares—twelve players, if possible, in six pairs. The trumpet players should not leave the stage until the general exodus of the women.

In Act III we have the two orchestras under the stage, one on the right and the other on the left. A transference of beat to the two off-stage conductors is an absolute necessity here. The weird and uncanny sound produced by these two orchestras of wind players and percussion answering one another and complementary to one another is wild in the extreme. Lastly there are the four trombones with the older Pilgrims on page 354 (full score). I cannot impress too strongly on the young conductor the necessity of expert transference of beat. Anything else than perfect ensemble during off-stage music effects will sound amateurish in the extreme. There are some people who think they know better and try to dispense with transference of beats but the result, if not disastrous, is generally unsatisfactory from the conductor's point of view. I have known conductors who revel in the process of catching up or waiting for the tempo inequalities of some off-stage conductors, but to the sensitive listener such practices are execrable and most painful.

Transference of beats has and always will be a most difficult problem. Various mechanical aids have been tried, but mostly with distressing results. Often a loud-speaker from the orchestral microphone will pick up extraneous noises: often the electrician will overload the circuit and a high-pitched "hum" is the only result. An electric sign (1, 2, 3, 4) actually controlled by the conductor has been tried but this doesn't allow for subdivision of beat and is therefore useless. There is only one way which is safe and sure—the human method.

It is always advisable that an assistant should listen to the balance while these final rehearsals are taking place. He should move about the auditorium and report immediately to the conductor any inequalities. He must remember one thing, however: that an empty auditorium is not quite the same thing as when the public fills it. Also during the preliminary stage rehearsals, when all the scenery is not being used and there is not enough "backing" for the voices with the result that the sound doesn't travel over the footlights, the assistant must make a mental mote of the bad places where balance seems to be uneven. If he finds that with the full scenery some of these places are still bad he should then inform the conductor.

The conductor should expect full co-operation from everyone at the final general rehearsal. Singers must sing full voice and act as if it were a real performance. The stage technical staff must show that they have fully grasped and solved all scenery and lighting problems.

At the end of the rehearsal the conductor should say a few words of encouragement to singers and orchestra and thank them for their part in building up the possibility of a perfect performance. For good or ill the final rehearsals are over and everyone must "gird up their loins" for the glorious experience of a first night.

Chapter XXIX

NUANCE: DYNAMICS

I HAVE often asked myself the reason why Verdi, particularly in *Aïda*, *Otello* and *Falstaff*, as well as in the last choral pieces, wrote such an excessive number of *p*s. Frequently in these latter works one finds *pppppp*. Such a dynamic does not exist. I doubt whether it is possible to extend the range of quantity of tone beyond *ff* or diminish it below *pp*. Then why Verdi's excessive exaggeration? The answer may well be that he was never satisfied with his singer's ideas or performance of the simple dynamics which he wrote in his earlier works, and to draw attention to these simple markings he wrote in this exaggerated way. Possibly the singers of his day could only sing with full voice and this exasperated him. Whatever the reason, Verdi committed a musical absurdity in exaggerating his dynamics. One finds however that he seems to have been troubled mostly about *pp* for it is mostly in soft passages he is given to exaggeration.

The subject bristles with difficulties. A singer who trains his or her voice to comply as far as possible with Verdi's markings may succeed in giving a drawing-room performance to the family circle but—and here is the difficulty—the same performance of dynamics would be fatal in an opera house during an operatic performance where the singer is accompanied by a large orchestra.

Let us begin by being realistic about the whole question. *p* means soft: *pp* means half as soft again: *ppp* must therefore mean almost inaudible. Apart from this we have the dynamic *mp* which means not quite as soft as *p*. It can all be very confusing unless an artist or a conductor has decided in his or her mind the amount of tone required in order to be *heard* under any circumstances. As we are discussing this question relative to performance in an opera house the conductor particularly must make up his mind so that he will be able to correct an artist's understanding of the whole subject.

The chief desire of the artist is to be heard by the audience. More often than not this results in an even f tone from beginning to end, thus robbing music of one of its most valued factors. Quality and quantity of tone are two of the most important factors of an artist's performance. There are many others, of course. Given good quality to tone, quantity becomes of the utmost importance. The artist can be helped by an understanding conductor and a sympathetic body of instrumentalists. But an inartistic singer, on the contrary, can bore an orchestra till all feeling for dynamics fades away. It is the duty of the conductor to prepare the ground orchestrally so that the singer will be encouraged to observe the composer's markings.

There is a magic about dynamics with its endless variation and subtle changes of colour which, if used to the full, can give thrilling pleasure to the listener. Climax in interpretation can be heightened to such an extent by this wise use of dynamics that excessive fatigue and strain should be almost absent. This, of course, presupposes that the singer knows how to sing in the first place.

Returning to the original discussion as to quantity of tone, how then can a singer know what p really means? The only answer possible is that a singer can only sing as softly as will enable him or her to be heard above the tone of the orchestra and by the audience, especially those (keenest of all) in the far-off gallery. Orchestral texture has a lot to do with it. Composers sometimes write for a combination of instruments marking them pp when the combined sound of these instruments in real life is much louder. A repetiteur will do well to point out to the singer when coaching, that whereas a pianoforte can be played pp (especially with the left pedal down) the particular combination of instruments for which the composer has scored that self-same passage (marking them all pp) will sound considerably stronger and that therefore the singer must use more tone.

A composer who seldom makes mistakes about balance of tone as between orchestra and singer is Massenet and the young conductor or operatic composer will find his operas of the utmost value for the purpose of studying this vexed question.

Puccini on the other hand frequently overloads his orchestration, again and again doubling the voice part and indeed obscuring it. There are a number of bars at the end of Act I of *La Bohème* ("Lovely Maid in the Moonlight", etc.) where the orchestra is marked *fff* and the voices *f*. In this place I have always contended Puccini intended these markings. The voices are treated as part of the orchestra. Conductors would make a great mistake if they attempted to water down Puccini's markings in those bars. But it is of other places in his operas that I feel Puccini is inclined to overload, sometimes with too heavy an orchestration, and at other times with an unsuitable combination of instruments for the type of voice and register. Sometimes he has been forced to put an unnatural diminuendo in the orchestral parts (but has often made a virtue of it) so that the voice at that moment descending to its lowest register can be heard. Massenet on the other hand is a master of orchestral-vocal balance. But aren't nearly all the French operatic composers? I can guarantee to the young conductor that if he follows out Massenet's dynamics any voice worthy enough will be heard without difficulty. Gounod is another expert at orchestral-vocal balance. It is with the moderns that this question of balance becomes a major issue. Mostly with Wagner and composers since Wagner does one experience difficulty. Humperdinck's *Hansel and Gretel* is piteously overscored and indeed in places wrongly scored for the voice. Humperdinck's love of the horns and cor anglais with oboes and bassoons manufactures a thick unwieldy texture like glue.

But what can a conductor do with these works? Their value as music is inestimable and to rescore them would take away the composer's individuality and possibly ruin them. I wonder what those opera-goers would say—those people who continually complain "the orchestra drowned the singer"—if one attempted to rescore operas to suit singers! A watered-down version of a composer's orchestration is a musical crime; yet one sighs for a solution of the problem.

The answer to it all may be in the value of the work of a repetiteur. He must be conversant enough with the orchestral texture to tell a singer that a *pp* written in the pianoforte part of a vocal score will sound much louder played by the orchestra and that therefore more tone is required than that marked by the composer in certain places in an opera. The conductor likewise will insist on those places being played by the orchestra as quietly as possible. All this is contingent upon the singer being able to sing with sufficient tone, and being rightly cast for the rôle. There is no solution to the problem otherwise.

The whole question therefore boils down to the *relative* value of a composer's markings. Generally speaking a *pp* played by the string orchestra is much softer than that played by a combination of wind players. *It is the composer's intention that matters.* He wants at times a colour of sound, *pp*, that strings cannot give; he writes *ppp* and in his mind he imagines a very quiet sound; he writes *ppp* for the singer, but invariably the singer and the words will be swamped. Certain wood-wind instruments either in their very high or very low registers cannot play quieter than *mf*. Composers frequently make the mistake of writing *ppp* for a piccolo in its highest octave. This is well-nigh impossible for most players of that instrument. An oboe on its bottom C or C♯ can only play *mf*. An orchestra is comprised of many players with many different makes of instruments. The old Buffé bassoon is still in use with its coarse lower register. In an ideal world with money unlimited it might be possible to insist on certain makes of instruments giving uniformity of tone (even this may be impossible because instruments of the same make often show dissimilar characteristics) but this is at the moment a hopeless dream.

Taking into consideration the many difficulties of balance mentioned above, the singer has a great task in the understanding of dynamics in opera. But even with these difficulties to contend with a clever singer, using a modicum of common sense, can work out a scheme of dynamics which will give him or her a good enough range of quantity of tone in any rôle. Helped by an experienced repetiteur, nursed by a good and knowledgeable conductor, there are immense possibilities for a satisfactory performance.

The experienced conductor has learnt by his work the kind of combination of instruments likely to cover up the voice and the singer will do well to listen to the voice of experience when studying a rôle.

Having explained, somewhat unscientifically, the difference between a *pp* as written and scored orchestrally by operatic composers and the actual sound as it reaches the listener, with the balance of the singer, also expected by the composer to sing *pp*, often against a strong (as in Puccini) orchestral combination, it is only a natural step forward to consider the acoustics of an opera house.

Before doing this, however, let us delve a little deeper into various combinations of instruments and their power of sound in combination.

The following table[1] will be of interest in the discussion of this point.

Source of Sound	Power in Watts (maximum)
Orchestra of seventy-five performers	70
Bass drum	25
Snare drum	12
Cymbals	10
Trombone	6
Bass tuba	0.2
Double bass	0.16
Orchestra of seventy-five at average loudness (probably *p*)	0.09
Piccolo	0.08
Flute	0.06
Clarinet	0.05
Horn	0.05
Triangle	0.05
Bass Voice	0.03
Alto voice (*pp*)	0.001
Average speech	0.000024
Violin (*ppp*)	0.0000038

It will be seen even with this incomplete table that a combination of flutes, clarinets, oboes, bassoons, horns, at their maximum loudness will always overwhelm the human voice at its maximum loudness. Likewise such a combination of instruments will also overwhelm the human voice singing when the minimum of strength is used.

If a singer using a vocal score insists that the composer

[1] From *The Physics of Music*, by Alexander Wood (Methuen).

(using an overwhelming combination of instruments in watts) has written *pp* both for the voice and instruments and that therefore the orchestra must sound *pp*, he or she is asking for an impossibility. If, on the other hand, a composer had in mind the relative power of the human voice in watts *pp* and scored for a combination of instruments which would sound (when added up together) *pp*, the question of balance would never arise. But few composers have studied the science of intensity of sound and are more concerned with the "colour" of their scoring and the musical atmosphere created and too frequently and blindly write *pp* for certain combinations which in the mass produce much more tone. The study of a score will reveal some very interesting inequalities in this respect. A combination of flutes, oboes, clarinets and horns all marked *pp* and playing the melody sung by the singer (as in numerous Puccini passages) whose part is also marked *pp*, as I have said before, is an impossibility of balance. The only remedy is that the singer *must* sing *mf* when his or her voice has to compete in intensity of sound and it is essential for the singer's words to be heard.

On the other hand looking at it from the orchestral player's point of view, he is not to blame if, playing his instrument *pp* as the composer directs (and the other instruments in the combination at that moment doing likewise), the aggregate amount of tone overwhelms the singer, singing *pp*.

So the conductor of opera or choral works has got to study this question of dynamics as applied to balance very seriously. He has to deal with the orchestra, the public, the singer, and last, but very important none the less, the acoustics of the opera house or hall.

The Orchestra

(a) The conductor will see to it that the players will faithfully perform their parts according to the composer's markings.

(b) He will make small alterations of dynamics where the balance is wrong; great care being taken that he doesn't "water down" the texture till all the inner intensity has been pruned out of the offending passages.

(c) He will also take care not to give way when the dramatic intensity is more orchestral than vocal as frequently happens in modern compositions.

(d) He will not give way when the singer chosen has not the right type of voice for the part. The remedy here is the right kind of voice. Where this is, for all sorts of reasons, not possible, then one has one of two choices: alter the dynamics all through, an almost impossible task unless time for rehearsal is arranged for, and further readjustment rehearsals when the right voice is found. Many people fondly imagine that this damping down of dynamics can be done at performance. One has only to remember how difficult this is when the biggest part of a musician's training has been to observe dynamics faithfully.

The Public

There are too many people who come to opera in order to listen only to the singer and not the composer's work. As a rule these people know very little of the orchestral score or the conditions under which it was written. Very often they don't even know the words or the story. They often don't realise the importance of the orchestra in the composer's mind. I must quote once again Puccini's scoring of the ninth bar of "Lovely Maid in the Moonlight", Act I, *La Bohème*. Here the composer has marked quite clearly *fff* for the orchestra and *f* for the singers. Obviously the watts of a full orchestra playing *fff* is going to overwhelm two singers singing *f*. There is no solution here (as in many other passages) and in a sense Puccini was absolutely right. It is the ecstasy and exultation of emotion and mood which he was trying to depict, a glorious wave of golden sound, and it is childish to babble about balance at this moment.

The Singer

Turandot is another case. If the Eva Turner type of voice is not available it is wiser to postpone a performance of this work. The same would apply to the *Ring* if a Flagstad or similar type of voice was not available. To water-down the orchestra for a smallish-voiced Brunhilde would be nonsense.

But singers should be coached by experienced coaches who know the places when the orchestral parts (and the vocal score) are marked *pp* but sound in the aggregate *mf* and all vocal scores re-marked to obviate instances of bad balance. Singers who "save" their voices only for the solos (and the

public's approbation) should be told that they must not
"throw away" what to them may seem to be unimportant
passages but which are in reality important from the dramatic
point of view. The singers who delight to sing *pp* "because the
composer has marked it so" would be well advised to go a little
deeper into the orchestral texture at these places so as to
safeguard themselves against being "drowned" by the
orchestra.

The Opera House or Hall and the Acoustics of Same

This is a very large subject, and a whole book could be
written about it. Suffice it to say here that the conductor must
be alive to the intensity of reverberation and length of the
echo of the building he is in. Often short *ff* chords have to be
damped if there is a sudden change of harmony following.
Again a comma may have to be inserted so that one sound can
die away before the next sound is played. The length of the
echo and intensity must be coped with in all sorts of ways. The
material with which orchestral pits are built will have a great
influence on the reverberation of the sound and different
instruments in certain register and notes will cause more
trouble than others. A lot will depend on the material used
for the walls of, and the shape of, the building. Hard materials
exaggerate echo and reverberation. Many of the older opera
houses mainly built of stone outside, but with the auditorium
covered with a porous material like limecast, have proved
ideal for sound absorption. A discussion on material used in
building our concert halls or opera houses, although somewhat out of place here, is, on the other hand, worth mention-
ing for the sake of a greater understanding of echo and
reverberation.

The question of the building of a perfect opera house or hall
is a matter of understanding the importance of three vital
elements in architecture: (a) cubic space per person; (b)
sound absorption factor in materials; and (c) resonance walls
and their angle (this involves the question of shape as well).

In regard to (a), from experiments and measurements in
existing halls where acoustics are good, a hundred and thirty
cubic feet per person in the auditorium is considered to be
proportionate.

Regarding (b), the best halls have a reverberation time of 4.4 seconds (approximately) when empty and 2.4 seconds when moderately full and 1.2 seconds when completely full. Opera houses, on the other hand, have a slightly shorter echo time-lag, which is in many respects a good thing for the reason that clarity is required when words are used. The fact that most opera houses have a quicker echo is mainly brought about by the materials used in the auditorium—cushion, wood, etc.—which have a high absorption value.

Finally in (c), the position and shape of echo walls is of the utmost importance. Convex or concave walls, the latter concentrating the echo in a small area and the former weakening it over a larger area, are mostly unsatisfactory. The most suitable are flat surfaces which, as with a mirror, reflect in a straight line.

It has been found possible, taking into consideration *all* these factors, to plan a hall or opera house which will have perfect acoustics for *the kind of performance desired*, be it concert hall or opera house.

So the principles of absorption, individual space and shape (including echo walls) will determine the success of performance from the musician's point of view. The understanding of these principles will give the conductor a ready-made appreciation of the kind of rehearsal required for a successful performance, or at least it will help him to solve the vexed question of the effect on the ears of his audience.

Summing up this section, I wish to put a point of view which may be of use to our singers. Some singers have an instinctive sense of the value of acoustics in a hall or opera house. I have even noticed that a singer will quickly adjust his or her voice in a matter of seconds, finding out in a flash of intuition the weak and strong points of a building and will alter the timbre of the voice accordingly. On the other hand, other singers will go blindly on, singing in the same way as they would in any old hall and afterwards they will rightly or wrongly blame the orchestra or conductor for being overwhelmed or for not being heard by their friends in the gallery. In some cases they are right but very often they fail to assess the cause. Singers must assess the acoustics of the building and use their voices accordingly. Producers of opera should also understand the difficulties of this problem by putting their singers in the right position on the stage where, in a particularly difficult ensemble, a certain voice *must* be heard.

Scenery also makes a great difference. The use of the cyclorama—a great blessing to designers—can at times be responsible for the loss of reflecting surfaces on the stage. All these things are worth a great deal of study.